Who's Calling the Shots?

Who's Calling the Shots?

How to Respond Effectively to Children's Fascination with War Play and War Toys

NANCY CARLSSON-PAIGE
DIANE E. LEVIN

New Society Publishers
Philadelphia, PA   Gabriola Island, BC

Inquiries regarding requests to reprint all or part of *Who's Calling the Shots?* should be
addressed to New Society Publishers, 4527 Springfield Avenue, Philadelphia, PA, 19143.

ISBN Hardcover   USA 0-86571-164-X   CAN 1-55092-034-0
ISBN Paperback   USA 0-86571-165-8   CAN 1-55092-035-9

Printed in the United States of America on partially recycled paper by BookCrafters of
Fredericksburg, Virginia.

Cover art by Sonya Ormrod. Cover and book design by Tina Birky.
Permission is gratefully acknowledged to the Center on War and the Child, Eureka
Springs, Arkansas, for the use of the photographs on pages 57, 60, and 72.

To order directly from the publisher, add $2.50 to the price for the first copy, 75¢ each
additional. Send check or money order to:

In the United States: *In Canada:*
New Society Publishers   New Society Publishers/New Catalyst
4527 Springfield Avenue   PO Box 189
Philadelphia, PA 19143   Gabriola Island, BC VOR 1XO

New Society Publishers is a project of the New Society Educational Foundation, a
nonprofit, tax-exempt, public foundation in the United States, and of the Catalyst
Education Society, a nonprofit society in Canada. Opinions expressed in this book do not
necessarily represent positions of the New Society Educational Foundation, nor the
Catalyst Education Society.

Table of Contents

Acknowledgments

Many people have played a part in the creation of this book. There are some who contributed in very specific ways, and others who were always available to help with the many problems that emerged from the beginning to the end of the whole project—from finding out about grassroots community actions on war toys, to helping us find the right publisher, to being willing to contribute their ideas in discussions about the many philosophical questions raised in this book. To all of these friends, we wish to express our deep appreciation. Specifically, they include:

—The hundreds of teachers and parents who gave us their time and shared their valuable insights with us.

—The many children who managed to forget that we were there watching them play, and who contributed their artwork to our collection of wonderful things made by children: Zachery Bowen, Kyle and Matthew Damon, Ian Joseph, Gregg Kline, Sametta Lam, Eli Levin-Goldstein, Andrew and Suzannah McLellan, Stefan Noble, Sonya Ormrod, Miguel Porcayo, Tom Targett, Collins and Ciel Wendell, and the children in Janice Danielson's Kindergarten.

—Their parents who put forth so much effort helping us observe and making sure we got everything we needed.

—The many friends who had us on their minds enough to send the steady stream of articles from the news that they had found, as well as the stories about children and commercial violence that were part of their own lives.

—Laura Schulman, Gail Willett and the Wheelock College Faculty Centennial Grants for the assistance they gave us in developing resources for using children's books as an alternative to television in promoting dramatic play.

—Amy Raffety for her assistance editing the early stages of the manuscript, and Michelle Pine for sharing her classroom activities.

—Gary Goldstein, Jay Jones, Sherry Langdale, Jeff Wein and Howard Zinn for their advice, assistance, and support.

—Zel Draz for her interest in our work and her generous support.

—Lesley College and Wheelock College for reducing our faculty responsibilities in order to allow time for us to do this work, and for providing environments in which our work can grow.

—And last but hardly least, our editor, Dave Albert, whom we have never seen face-to-face, but feel we have come to know . . . for his immediate enthusiasm for this book, and unyielding cheerfulness and clear-mindedness throughout the editing process; and the many people at New Society Publishers who made all the arduous tasks required for finalizing this book seem pleasant.

Publisher's Note

Parenting, or so I imagine, is not what it used to be. I imagine there was a time when parents of young children, like myself, could go to their elders for advice and guidance concerning specific problems which came up in the course of interactions with their children. And elders could reflect on their own experience, and that of those who went before them, and offer words of wisdom based on confidence in the experience of past generations, knowing that these specific situations had been faced before, and dealt with successfully.

We live in dangerous times, times where the pace of change is so accelerated that many of the problems for which parents might look to their elders for advice simply didn't exist when members of the past several generations were growing up. My own grandfather, for example, grew up in a village without electricity no less automobiles, without public education no less television. What to do about paper diapers, given our contemporary problems of waste disposal, would never have been a question; the idea of modern diaper services would not likely have appeared in a culture without washing machines.

We now accept political suffrage as part of our birthrite, and assume that others without it must be sorely oppressed. Yet, social choices concerning the uses of technology, to a large part the engine behind so many of the changes we have witnessed in our lifetimes, is still viewed as beyond our sovereignty. In fact, there is barely public recognition, and virtually none voiced by our politicians or educators, that such choices exist at all. One would almost think we are hostages to our own tools, that placing limits on any of the technologies barely dreamed about even a hundred years ago—from automobiles spewing fumes into the air to agricultural pesticides poisoning our waters—would symbolize that we are somehow less "free" than our contemporary Promethean mythology can allow us to admit.

I am old enough to remember educators in the '50s waxing poetic about how television technology would revolutionize our lives by providing mass education—"bringing the world into our living rooms" as they were wont to say—virtually twenty-four hours a day. They were correct of course, though not in ways they imagined.

The average television viewer in North America watches twenty-three hours of television a week, some four-and-a-half of which is made up of commercial advertising. Not that the non-commercial programming is very different; one of the distinguishing features between the non-commercial programming and the advertising is that the commercial segments name the brands being conspicuously consumed on the shows themselves.

Most children watch substantially more. Upon graduation from high school, young adults will have spent as many as 25,000 hours in front of the television set, significantly more time than in the classroom, and may have received through this medium as many as 350,000 commercial messages. And just as the differences between commercial and non-commercial programming are not that great, we should note that the differences between the classroom and the television room are usually overstated: in both cases, adults address impersonal and sometimes very "loaded" messages to large numbers of impressionable people. True, a teacher may deliver a "live" message and the television a recorded one, but on the other hand, the classroom may have as many as forty "receivers," while the television room only one or two who, at least in theory, have chosen this pursuit voluntarily.

Today's defenders of television (and, thankfully, there are now fewer and fewer educators among them), in contrast to their enthusiastic counterparts of the '50s, argue that it has very little if any effect on social behavior, and cannot be held responsible for aberrant social behavior. The apologists don't of course really believe their own argument; if they did, they wouldn't be able to sell commercial time. Although this fact is entirely absent from our textbooks, ours is the first age in the history of civilization in which so many thousands of the best trained minds have made it their full-time occupation to manipulate the public will, and translate it into social behavior. They may not do so directly in the name of a totalitarian state, but they certainly do so in the name of consumerism—our virtually sacrosanct and unchallenged civic religion. In an age in which "news" is virtually defined as that which reaches us through the televised medium, it is not surprising to watch our civic culture, if not our civil liberties as well, reduced to little more than consumer choices, whether among the major networks, the major parties, or among the advertised brands.

At one level, *Who's Calling the Shots?* is about the new generation of war toys and their television tie-ins, the effects of these toys on our children, and what we can do about them. But if there is a larger message to be inferred from *Who's Calling the Shots?* it is that we must find a way to fight to regain democratic and community control over technological choices. Without that control, our ballot box freedoms amount to little more than choices among breakfast cereal boxes, our freedom of speech protecting little more than coffee-table conversation. The evidence of media manipulation of our children and its negative effects presented in this book is overwhelming; the outstanding question, really, is how we, as parents, are able to do as good a job as we do in raising our children, given the social and technological forces we are up against?

Who's Calling the Shots? leaves us with a hopeful message as well. In a culture of increasing violence and manipulation, we can find ways to reclaim our stake in the future, through our children, but also for ourselves. It is this message of hope, presented to us as parents and teachers, but also as the elders of tomorrow's generations, which makes us at New Society Publishers proud to publish *Who's Calling the Shots? How to Respond Effectively to Children's Fascination with War Play and War Toys.*

David H. Albert
Santa Cruz, California
24 October, 1989

Dedication

For our parents

Peg and John
Emma and Arthur

Thank-you for valuing our play
and for the cap guns and cowgirl boots.

And for our children

Eli, Kyle and Matthew

You are our greatest resource.

Introduction

In the fall of 1982, the organizer of a conference, "Helping Children and Families Live in the Nuclear Age," came to us. He had been unable to find any "experts" who knew about how the nuclear threat might affect young children. He hoped we might be able to come up with something useful to share with conference participants in an afternoon workshop.

We agreed to give the workshop a try, because we had a longstanding interest in children's political and moral development, and because we didn't want young children to be left out of this topic which was receiving increasing attention all around the country. Between us we had many years of experience working with young children and teaching teachers of young children. And, we were both parents. Nancy's two sons were entering adolescence at the time, and Diane, with a two-month-old son, was just beginning to see how her career in child development would match up with real parenting.

As we began to look for material for the workshop, we realized that in the growing body of writing about the effects of the nuclear threat on children and adolescents, children under the age of six or seven years were almost completely left out. Fortunately, a group of teachers of young children in the Boston area who belonged to Educators for Social Responsibility were collecting information about how children's knowledge of war and the nuclear threat was surfacing in their classrooms. Their written accounts (often of play episodes or drawings) gave us an invaluable place to begin. The examples intrigued us; the more we looked at them, the richer and more interesting they became. We could see how the children, each in their own unique ways, were trying to make sense of the social and political world around them. We got hooked on trying to make sense of their understanding and ended up writing a book about what we learned, *Helping Young Children Understand Peace, War and the Nuclear Threat*.

Little did we know then that we had started down a path—one which would lead us into in-depth study of many aspects of children's political development, and into an intense professional collaboration which would evolve and deepen for what has now been seven years and is still going strong. Throughout these years, the course of our work has changed, but its direction has always been mapped by parents and teachers, from whom we are always finding out what needs to be studied next.

Seven years ago, we did not think war play was particularly connected to children's understanding of war and peace. As early childhood educators, we were coming from a child development tradition. We felt that war play was one valuable way children met their deep developmental needs. It didn't seem to us that war play had much to do with violence in the real world. Although as teachers of young children we had limited war play in our classrooms, mostly for practical reasons, we were not opposed, in principle, to allowing it. As a former play therapist, Diane had seen the power of war and superhero play in helping troubled children work out their feelings of anger and helplessness. Nancy had watched her son Matthew's passionate and long-term involvement in war play begin when he was three (as she was going through a divorce) and last in different forms until he was at least twelve. She saw both Matthew and his brother Kyle, who played war and superhero games together, develop nonviolent attitudes and hopes for world peace as they grew older.

Our developmental bias caused us to turn a deaf ear to the first questions we heard from parents and teachers who asked how war play and war toys fit in with children's political and moral understanding. But at the workshops we gave during the mid eighties, the questions began coming with increasing frequency and there was a growing sense of urgency about them. Many teachers were saying that children seemed obsessed with war play in a way they had not seen in the past, and that they were seeing more violent play.

After about a year of hearing these concerns, we decided it might help people alleviate them if we were to write an article explaining the developmental value of war play. But we decided to start this project by studying war play more systematically. We sent out questionnaires, conducted interviews, and observed many children at play. We had no idea that what we thought would be a short project would turn into four years of research and two books, first *The War Play Dilemma: Balancing Needs and Values in the Early Childhood Classroom,* and now this book. Nor did we expect that our own ideas about war play would change so dramatically.

What we learned from our research was truly upsetting. Slowly we began to realize that our original view was far too simplistic. Our point of view began to change. We had to modify some of our early assumptions, and there were times when this was an extremely uncomfortable process for both of us.

The teachers and parents had been right. There *was* something to worry about. The war play they had been describing to us was not a simple case of developmental needs being met in a new contemporary context. Many other factors were playing a potentially negative role in children's play, and thus, perhaps in their development as well.

What we have learned about war play and what we write about in this book comes from several sources. First, we are not just armchair theorists. In addition to having taught young children ourselves, our own experiences as parents have been of tremendous importance to our work. On a daily basis, Diane has been struggling to find constructive approaches for dealing with almost every issue associated with contemporary war play discussed in this book. Nancy brings her years of experience with her sons' war play and where their interests and her efforts have taken all three of them over time. It is, to a large extent, from her experience that we have come to appreciate how much the war play and war toy scene has changed in the last ten years. Secondly, we have relied heavily on the accounts of literally hundreds of parents and teachers. Without their willingness to talk openly with us about their thoughts and feelings, successes and failures, we could never have written this book. Third, while we have found very little in early childhood literature specifically about war play, we attempt to use general ideas from child development theory, research and practice. Wherever possible, we utilize ideas about the general stages of political, intellectual and moral development and about play and the media—to create a framework for understanding the war play culture of today.

The views we express here and the suggestions we make grow out of our basic assumptions about play in general. One is that play is crucial to children's healthy development. A second is that children show us through the things they choose to play with what issues they need to work on. Third is that children use their play as a way of making sense of the experiences they have. Finally, we assume children learn things as they play, and the content and quality of their play determines what they will learn. And, it is especially with this last point that we think parents have a crucial role to play.

Following these assumptions, we present a point of view about war play which many of you may find difficult to accept. We argue that in the current social climate, parents should not try to ban war play. Not only is it next to impossible to do so when children are bombarded by violent images in their daily lives (as they are today), but banning one kind of play or another ignores a fundamental aspect of healthy development—children *need* to be in control of what they play. And we believe it does children a disservice to cut them off from a form of play that is well-suited to help them work through their thoughts and feelings about the increasing amounts of violence they see.

But we also argue that simply allowing war play would be a big mistake. The play culture currently offered to American children, the whole context in which war play takes place, has changed dramatically in recent years. Forces outside the home are affecting children and their war play in ways we are only beginning to understand. What is clear to us now is that parents and children are losing control of war play and war toys. Television and the marketing strategies of large corporations are playing a greater and greater role. It seems to us that this change has greatly increased the chances that war play will have negative effects on children. So parents need to find ways to influence their children's involvement in war play and help them regain some of the control they have lost.

We want to be sure we don't make parents feel that the responsibility for what is happening with war play today is theirs alone. Parents are frequently blamed for *allowing* their children to become involved with war play and war toys. We know the discomfort this can cause. Diane frequently gets incredulous looks from friends and colleagues when they see her son Eli running around pretending to shoot everything in sight or fondling a toy weapon. The current situation is not the fault of parents nor is it fair to place the burden of controlling the situation on them. The play culture that is offered to children, and the media and toys that are part of it, should be issues of national, public concern. But we have a very long way to go. There are only the beginnings of public awareness and debate concerning these issues in the United States. In the last chapter of this book, "Calling the Shots," we discuss what we can do to make children's play a legitimate focus of public debate and policy.

In the meantime, until we can change the societal forces influencing war play, we have written this book to help parents become more informed about their children's interest in war play, so they can reclaim some of the influence that is their right to have over their own children's play and development.

We begin in Chapter One, "The Times They Are A Changin'," by taking a careful look at the changing context for war play. We look at changes like the deregulation of children's television and the link-up between TV shows and toy lines, and their consequences for parents and children.

In the next two chapters we provide a framework for understanding the potential value of play (Chapter Two, "Before the Three R's") and war play (Chapter Three, "Bang! Bang! You're Dead!"). We point out the qualities that characterize rich and meaningful play and consider when both play generally, and war play specifically, might and might not be serving their optimal role in development. The framework established in these chapters will equip parents to look at and understand their own children's war play and to identify where they might begin to play a role in it.

In Chapter Four, "From Sticks and Stones to Lasers," we look at the role of toys in war play and how the newest generation of war toys can channel children into violent play and undermine the potential value of that play.

Chapter Five, "Mama Won't You Buy Me A GI Joe?" explores how marketing techniques have changed in recent years and why they are so effective at manipulating children to respond to their messages. Much of the discussion in this chapter responds to the frustrations many parents feel over consumer pressure on their children.

Chapter Six, "Whatever Happened to Annie Oakley?" looks at the heightened divisions in girls' and boys' play and the toys they use. It addresses the commonly asked question, "Why is war play almost entirely a male issue?" and describes how many of the same negative forces affecting war play also have a detrimental impact on play common among girls.

In Chapter Seven, "Learning About War; Learning About Peace," we turn to what we see as the all important "bottom line"—how the picture of contemporary war play we have drawn up to this point affects the political lessons children are learning. We look at the actual messages about the world that are supplied to children via television and marketing, how these messages have different meanings for children than for adults, and how such messages can affect children's views of the world.

And, in the eighth chapter, "Calling the Shots," we look at the bigger picture of public policy, social responsibility and action steps that have been, can and should be taken.

Trying to raise young children in a society that encourages war and weapon play and which offers few support systems for childrearing can leave many parents feeling overwhelmed. So instead of just pointing to the serious problems we see with war play today, we try in this book to help parents discover specific ways to counteract the destructive forces, and to foster children's healthy development and play in the midst of a troubled and troubling situation. We do this by providing practical suggestions at the end of each chapter for how parents can start to implement positive approaches to the issues addressed in that chapter. Many of the solutions suggested come from parents we have talked to as well as from our own experiences as parents. Then, in Part II, we provide a wealth of additional ideas and resources which can further assist children in developing positive and fulfilling play.

This kind of a book is full of suggestions for parents but few foolproof answers. Some suggestions will match you and your child's individual situation and be helpful, others will not. Try them out, use those that work for you, and don't worry if some simply don't seem to meet your or your child's particular needs. The last thing we want is to contribute to the guilty feelings many parents already have about not doing their job well enough. Instead, we hope the ideas we offer in this book will be taken as a set of possibilities that can be tried here and there, that provide readers with a new sense of empowerment. And we also hope that the ideas will help parents better appreciate and enjoy their children's play.

One final note—in contemporary America, it is boys more than girls who are involved in war play. We are aware, however, of girls (more rare than in the past) who have an equal interest and passion for war play along with boys. These girls are very special, and bring diversity and individuality to the contemporary play scene. But because, as mentioned earlier, the vast majority of war players are boys, we feel that it is more authentic to use male pronouns when discussing war play, and to use female pronouns when the discussion topics include greater numbers of girls.

PART I
War Play in Perspective

1
The Times
They Are a Changin'
War Play Today

When my son Eli was almost three years old, he and I (Diane) were out for a neighborhood walk. We saw a five-year-old boy in his garden holding a large plastic imitation "machine gun." When he pulled the trigger, it made a loud noise and a red light at the end flashed. As we walked by, the boy kept pulling the trigger without paying much attention. Eli slowed down to take a careful look. As we began to walk away, we had the following conversation:

> Eli: I want one of those.
> Diane: One of what?
> Eli: One of those.
> Diane: Do you mean you want a toy like the boy had?
> Eli: Yes.
> Diane: What do you think the toy is?
> Eli: I don't know. (pause) Maybe it's a gun.
> Diane: What would you do with it if you had one?
> Eli: I *want* one.

We have heard so many stories like this from parents. For many, their young children's fascination with toy weapons and pretend shooting from one or two chance exposures is proof that war play is of universal interest to children. But, while this is a common belief, we don't really have enough evidence to know whether or not it is true.

We do know that people have long pondered why war play is so fascinating to many children. For instance, at the beginning of the twentieth century the British writer Saki* wrote a short story called "Toys of Peace" in which he considers what would happen to children's play if they were given toys of peace instead of toys of war. We know that even in the last century, debates occurred about the possible effects

---

*Saki. *The complete works of Saki*. London: The Bodley Head, 1980.

9

of exposing children to even fictional violence; in nineteenth-century Britain the violence in classic fairy tales became the focus of a heated public dialogue. And we know that war play has been around for a long time—artifacts of what might be war toys have been found from ancient Egypt and the Middle Ages (see Chapter Four)—and that it occurs among children in many countries around the world.

But it seems to us that what has changed over time may be at least as important as what has remained the same. In American society today, children (mostly boys) play war with GI Joe and Evil Mutant action figures, Cobra killer vehicles and weapons which claim to be able to destroy or save the world with a single pull of the trigger. They act out violent dramas they have seen on television with characters and equipment which encourage them to replicate those dramas. Many adults who watch war play wonder if it is the same as in the olden days, only with modern-day themes and toys. Some worry about how violent the play seems, how ubiquitous, and how tied up the play is with violent toys and television. And some ask whether children are learning the same lessons from their play as they did in the past.

What's Different Now?

War play today exists in a context which is very different from any in times past. What we are providing children and the way we are providing it has changed dramatically. Today, it is no longer simply a matter of children's particular themes or toys reflecting society; societal forces in the form of media and toy companies have become major influences in the promotion of specific forms of children's play.

Over and over, in our conversations with parents and teachers and in our observations of children's play, television surfaced as an all-pervasive influence. Television, after all, has only been around for fifty years. We were the first generation raised on TV. Now over 97 percent of all US households have at least one television set. Young children watch an average of four hours of TV a day. They are likely to see thousands of acts of violence and thousands of ads each year. What they see reflects a set of social values which may not be those of their parents and is often a white, middle-class, "all-American" world which may not look like the one they know. And independent of the content of what they see on TV, children sit passively glued to it, unable to affect what happens in any way except by turning the knobs. They are taken away from other things they could be doing, should be doing and have been doing for generations before the advent of television—like playing, interacting with other children and participating in family and community life. It's often difficult to separate out issues of war play from issues associated with television.

Before television was so important and so all-pervasive, the themes children used in war play grew out of their direct experiences and their deep personal needs. Today much of the content is coming from TV script writers' ideas about what children will watch. At no other time in history have children had daily exposure to so many images removed from direct experience, many of which focus on violence. Children's television offers far more hours of war cartoons than it did just a few years ago (more than twenty-seven hours a week in 1988 as compared to one and a half hours a week in 1982). As of September, 1987, a child could buy an expensive toy which, when used along with a television show, would "interact" electronically in a shooting match with the television set.

So, not only children's television, but the toys used in war play are changing. They are playing an increasingly important role in shaping war play. There is a proliferation of war toys on the market, most of which are linked to the television shows children watch. The sale of war toys has risen by over 500 percent in the last four years, to well over a billion dollars a year. The best-selling toy over the Chistmas season for the past several years has been some kind of war toy. Supermarkets, toy stores and department stores carry all kinds of products which bear the same violent images children see on cartoons.

As will be described throughout this book, these changes are affecting the very nature of war play today, and not for the better. Some of the changes have crept up gradually, for instance, the amount of time children spend watching television. But something new has happened in recent years, something that most of us didn't even pay attention to until we began seeing the effects on children and their play.

Children's TV Becomes a Free-for-All

The media and toy culture presented to children has changed dramatically in the 1980s. The changes are a direct result of changes in federal regulations under the Reagan administration. Over a six-year period, the Federal Communications Commission, which governs the television industry, gradually nullified most of the FCC regulations that once tried to assure quality programming for and control advertising aimed at children. Perhaps the most important regulations eliminated were those that prevented the sale of toys connected to television shows. Prior to the 1980s, the Commission had said that programming should come first, not the selling of products; that it was illegal to market a toy that was also a televison show. They also placed a limit on the number of advertising minutes per hour permitted on children's television. But during the Reagan era, the FCC moved to deregulate the broadcasting industry. In 1984, it eliminated the advertising time restrictions. It also ruled that product-based shows were legal. These rule changes made the "program-length commercial," the marketing of toys as part of the programs, legal for the first time.

The result was that the toy and television industries quickly joined together in their marketing efforts. They developed toys that were directly linked with cartoon programs. Toy manufacturers got into the business of making children's TV shows for the first time as they began developing the toys and programs as a package. They developed whole lines of toys that children could use to act out what they saw on television. The profits in toy sales were enormous and some toy manufacturers began to share the wealth with television stations that carried their shows. By December of 1985, all of the ten best-selling toys had television shows connected to them; and in the fall of 1987, 80 percent of all children's television programming was produced by toy companies.

Parents and Teachers See Changes in War Play

The effects of these changes were quickly felt by those who live closest to children—their parents and teachers. Almost immediately they began to notice how children's play and behavior were affected by the powerful and sophisticated marketing techniques aimed at them.

We continue to talk to hundreds of parents and teachers from around the country about their experiences with their children's war play. Many express their concerns, confusions and strong feelings to us. One father said, "The violence is everywhere, you can't get away from it. Sometimes I wonder, Maybe they're trying to get these kids prepared for war." A mother remarked, "When they play at the park, they get on the jungle gym and zap each other. They get in a machine gun pose, using their arms and hands. They don't have feelings about someone dying." And a daycare director told us, "I went and bought two beautiful new dolls and within two days two of the boys decapitated one of them and described in great detail that they had seen something like that on television."

As we talk to parents, their experiences and concerns focus on several central points. Children often seem obsessed with war play. They repeat the same violent acts or gestures over and over. It is often hard to get them to do anything else for long. They are bringing the violent behavior of their war play into other situations. Many parents give examples of children playing, at the park for example, when suddenly one child uses a stereotyped aggressive gesture and hits another child. And, almost every adult we talk to mentions the influence of television on the play—the characters, actions and scripts all originate in TV cartoons—which comes either from the children watching the shows themselves or from a friend who has watched.

Parents who are concerned about the effects of the recent changes in media and toys have legitimate worries. Children learn many important lessons as they play. As the media/toy culture has become an increasingly important influence on children and their war play, it is having a profound effect on play and on what children learn as they play.

War Play: Love It Or Leave It?

People who are one step removed from young children often say that parents should control the television programs their children watch and the toys they possess. They argue that when it comes to war play, it is up to parents to decide whether "to love it or leave it"; and, if today's parents are having a difficult time dealing with their children's war play and toys, it is their fault. Pointing the finger at parents for the difficulties they are having with their children is a common practice in society today. It is often the easiest way to deal with a problem, but it also ignores the complexities of that problem.

The many parents we talk to tell a disturbing story. They explain that it is hard to feel very good about anything they try. They are often exhausted and demoralized from having to argue so much with their children over television and playthings. They say that their efforts to deal with their children's war play are often ineffective. They find there are limits to what they can accomplish as parents when they have to struggle against the social forces which surround them. The following is the story we heard from Louise.

Louise:
Trying to draw the line on Nick's war toys is a constant struggle, and it gets worse by the minute. Every time he sees a friend with something new or when we're out at stores, there's something he wants. I feel like I have to be on my guard all the time.

He didn't really know about this stuff until he went to school, because I didn't let him watch the violent cartoon shows on TV. But he caught on really fast. One big incident was Will's birthday party. Nick was really excited about being invited. We talked about what would be a good present to get for Will, and decided on a nice set of scented felt-tip pens with a large blank jigsaw puzzle to decorate. Nick was real happy with this; he was beaming when I left him off at the party.

When I arrived for the pick-up a couple of hours later, Nick dragged me over to see the birthday presents saying, "Mom, Look what Will got!" He pointed to the largest box and said, "Can I have one of these too?" It was a "Cobra (GI Joe's enemy) Mamba Command Weapon."

I realized that nine of the eleven presents Will got were fighting toys representing at least six different toy lines from "Transformers" to "Star Com" toys. Nick's present was buried at the bottom of the heap.

On the way home in the car Nick started working on me to get him toys like Will's. He wanted to see if he could get anything out of me but he also seemed a bit desperate. I felt really uncomfortable and mad. I didn't want to get involved in the whole thing with him again. And I had this sinking feeling that the next time we needed to choose a birthday present it would be a real struggle.

The issue of war play and whether or not it is good for children is not new; it has been a concern of parents for generations. Yet at the same time, Louise's experience is different from that of parents who raised their children prior to the 1980s.

In the past, when parents watched their children make guns out of sticks and raw carrots, if they thought about it at all, it was usually in one of two general ways. There were parents who thought about gun play as a natural, even healthy, form of play. They watched their children's pleasure in playing out themes of good against evil, and surmised that something this satisfying to children must have value. They thought about the play as purely pretend—not having to do with events in the real world, but rather, coming from the needs and imaginations of children. These parents generally did not mind if their children pretended to play war, and rarely interfered with such play.

There were also parents who did not like to see their children fighting and "pretending" to hurt or kill others. They worried that war play would teach their children to be violent and would influence the attitudes and values they learned. These parents often refused to buy guns for their children and told them they could not play war at home.

Until recently, it was possible for parents to take whichever position was more comfortable and to implement it at home without much difficulty. Many parents did not even need to take a position because war play just was not a big issue for them. Those who did ban war play might occasionally have to remind their children of the ban. Those who allowed it sometimes had to state a limit or help their children calm down. Sometimes parents discussed or disagreed among themselves about these different views, but usually they felt quite comfortable about whichever approach they adopted and so did their children.

But with the rapid changes in the climate which influences children's play in the past few years, whether they begin with any strong views about war play or not, more and more parents are being pushed into taking a position. When they do they are finding that neither of the previously stated policies on war play is easy to implement. Whether they try to allow it or ban it, they end up wondering if they are taking the wrong approach, and many have changed their original position. They no longer say that whatever policy they choose to implement is working for them or for their children. In fact, many parents tell us that they have not found any approach that works as well as they would like:

Randy:

When Jamal was four and a half or five, he started asking for a He-Man figure. He showed us the figures in the store and he really wanted us to buy them for him. I said "no," that they were ugly, they were violent, all the things I hated about them. At that time he only watched Sesame Street and Mr. Rogers on television, but his cousin and friends were getting these toys. And for about six months, he kept on, "I want them, so and so has them . . . I want them . . . so and so has them . . . why won't you let me have them?" Then he slept at his cousin's house for a few days, and when I picked him up he had his own He-Man figure. They had bought him one, which I knew I could not take away. But then he wanted more. He wanted the bad guy to go with it; he wanted Skeletor to go with He-Man, this whole thing.

Cara:

Jacob says, "Mom, will you play GI Joe with me?" If I could find something else that he would like as much, where I wouldn't feel like I'm compromising my values, I would like that better. Right now, he would rather play GI Joe than anything else. I feel like I'm rejecting him if I say I won't do it. I know those GI Joe figures help him somehow. This morning he took one, a scuba diver, to school. I had said, "Why don't you take Raggedy Andy?" but he only wanted the GI Joe. He was sobbing out of control when I was leaving him at school and I said, "What will help you now?" He went and got his GI Joe figure. I feel like I'm fighting—all the commercials, the ingenious advertising, all the stuff at "Toys R Us," and I can't fight that. That stuff makes it more powerful for Jacob. I'm standing there holding this Raggedy Andy thinking, it doesn't cut the mustard. It doesn't do it, and I'm just not good enough to make it do it. I can't give it the power that those guys can give the GI Joe stuff.

The experiences of Louise, Randy and Cara reveal a lot about the difficulties parents have raising children in a climate which inundates them with images of violence and war. Children use their play as a way to make sense of their experience, so it's understandable that play today reflects the violence they see. Because violence in our society, especially in the media is so all-pervasive, it's not surprising children are often obsessed with war play. So parents can no longer simply allow war play and look the other way or ban it and be done with it.

When parents try to ban it, their children may often pursue the forbidden fruit behind their backs. Numerous parents tell of how their children try to sneak peaks at banned cartoons or get their hands on war toys at friends' houses, and in a few extreme cases, even try to steal a forbidden gun or toy from a friend or store. Some of the children we talk to also confess, with considerable anguish, to these deeds. There is a danger in making a young child feel guilty about the way he or she wants to play, and a risk in forcing a child into the position of sneaking access to what is popular and feeling guilty about it.

And, when parents openly allow war play, they usually find out they have opened a Pandora's Box which they are unable to close. Many report that their children become obsessed with war play and toys, that the cartoon heroes are on their minds constantly, as are ideas about what toy to get next. Many parents say their children's play seems to copy television shows and is very violent. They often worry that the violence is spilling out beyond the fantasy play into other situations.

But even if today's parents could just love war play or leave it behind, there is another reason why they shouldn't. It has to do with changes in the very nature of war play itself. In the past, children determined the content of their war play. They made guns out of whatever materials they could find and they invented pretend enemies using their imaginations. In doing so, they were in charge of their war play and the ideas they formed from it. As we shall see in the following chapters, they used their play in the service of their development. With the pressures that influence war play today, this often is no longer the case.

Finding a New Approach

Increasingly the media and toy industries have been taking the control of war play away from children. They are "calling the shots": determining much of the content of children's play and the lessons that are learned; they have become nothing short of major agents of socialization in children's lives. So if parents try to declare an all-out ban on war play and their children still do it, then parents may actually be taking themselves out of the situation and leaving it to the influence of outsiders. And if they freely allow war play and toys without intervening at all, they clear the way for the powerful media and toy industries to exert an untempered and perhaps detrimental influence over their children.

Old approaches to war play are not working and *cannot* work in the current climate. They do not take into account changes in society or the changing needs of children. Children and parents would both have an easier time and be better off if the violence that surrounds them were to disappear magically. But given that children are being raised in the social climate they are, we need to think about what to do.

This book raises some "seemingly intractable" issues about war play and war toys today. But our goal is to show that despite our concerns, there are many things we all can do to raise healthy, socially responsible children. We do this by forging an approach to war toys and war play that gets beyond allowing it or banning it, one which will help children reestablish control over their war play and move away from the central focus on violence.

2
Before the Three R's
Why Dramatic Play

Joey flies through the living room dressed in a superman cape and waving a jumprope. Angela sets up all of her small plastic animals in a circle and builds a fence "so the mean monster can't get them." It's probably hard to remember when either of them first tucked a toy animal into a pretend bed or crashed one toy figure into another. We get so used to seeing their fantasy play that it quickly becomes a regular part of our daily lives with young children. It seems so spontaneous and natural. Yet if we stop to think about it, this kind of play is nothing short of central to children's healthy development. It serves a profound purpose in their lives, that of helping them understand and master personal experience, ideas and feelings.

An endless variety of themes and actions will enter Joey's and Angela's pretend worlds before their early childhood years are over. It's likely that one of the themes will be war play. To gain an appreciation of war play and to understand how it is changing today, we'll begin by looking at the qualities of dramatic play that make it the powerful force it is in childhood.

Mario in the Kitchen: Learning Through Play

Mario, who recently had his fourth birthday, comes into the kitchen just as his father has put his baby sister, Rosa, in the highchair. He watches as his father puts a bib on Rosa, and prepares some hot cereal. Mario's father pulls a seat up to the highchair and begins to feed the baby. Mario leaves the kitchen for a minute and returns with his rubber dolly. He finds Rosa's infant seat on the floor and puts his doll in it. He looks at his father, then cups his left hand, scoops his right hand into it, and offers some pretend food to his doll.

After offering his doll a few scoops of food, Mario picks the doll up and goes into his room. There he sets the doll on the floor and begins to stack some large cardboard building blocks in a way that resembles a tall chair, then puts his doll in it. He fetches more blocks and builds a second chair similar to the first but with some arms and takes a small teddy bear from his bed and sets it in the second chair. He begins to hum. Mario gets a can of playdough and carefully pulls out some pieces, putting a handful on the plate in front of each doll. When each doll has some "food," Mario sits and surveys the situation. He adjusts the amount of food in front of each doll until it appears to be exactly the same. He reaches for the playdough in front of the teddy bear and mushes it all up in his hand and makes it into a big lump. Then he reaches for some crayons from a can. He sticks several of them into the playdough and starts to sing: "Happy Birthday to You . . . "

In this little scene, Mario is engaging in pretend or dramatic play. He takes a piece of his own personal experience—watching his father feed Rosa—and he transforms it into a unique creation of his own making. The course of the play is completely determined by Mario. It is a dynamic creation of many things—Mario's personal experience, his desires and imagination, his developmental needs, his ability to symbolize or to use an object to represent something else and his own special way of bringing all of these things together. No other child would create a scene exactly like this because the elements that go into play are unique to every child.

This small fifteen-minute scene, and many more like it throughout Mario's day, form one important basis for his healthy development. Dramatic play helps Mario to understand and master his experiences as he makes them over in his own terms. All of the play scenes that make up Mario's day continually help him to make sense of life and provide a basis for understanding the next experiences he will have. And they show us what he understands and what is important to him.

As we watch Mario, we can see that his play goes through some important changes from beginning to end. At first, he uses his doll to represent a real baby as he primarily copies what he saw his father doing. As he moves into his room and begins to build a chair, Mario is starting to change and elaborate the original feeding idea—he is creating his own feeding scene. As he starts to work on the second chair, he is introducing another variation—there is now room for a new character. He is really inventing a new story, with new roles and new props that he designs. As his play progresses, Mario brings in new elements from his own experience, such as his recent birthday party.

Mario is able to use his play to work on his own social, emotional and intellectual issues and work on them in his own way at his own developmental level. For example, as he distributes the playdough "food" evenly and fairly between his dolls, he is working on all three areas. On an intellectual level, he is learning about math concepts as he divides the playdough between the two dolls and tries to make sure they have the same amount. In the social and emotional areas, he is trying out the role of provider, and learning how to nurture and care for others. He is also gaining experience with the ideas of sharing and cooperation, something children his age struggle to comprehend and accept. Working on it in play can be much more meaningful to Mario than being told by his father to share a toy with his baby sister. Play also allows Mario to practice sharing while he has control—he can decide to share the playdough between his dolls if he chooses to, but no one is telling him he has to share.

At the height of his involvement, Mario is actively inventing a completely original scene. He is a playwright, actor and director all in one. He has a sense of mastery over the situation and a feeling of equilibrium as he integrates all the different elements that make up his own unique "production."

All Dramatic Play Is Not the Same: Play Versus Imitation

All of children's pretend play is not as rich and dynamic as Mario's. And when it is not, it does not contribute to development and learning in the ways we just saw. Imagine that instead of what actually did happen in Mario's play scene, the following scenario occurred:

Mario goes and gets his doll as before, and feeds her like his father feeds Rosa. Mario does this for a long time. Over and over he reaches for the pretend food and then offers it to his doll. Then, he watches his father clean off Rosa's hands and face and lift her from the highchair. Mario pretends to clean off his doll and then puts her into Rosa's now empty highchair. He retrieves Rosa's cereal dish from the sink and pretends to feed his doll once again, now using Rosa's dish. After some time, he seems to tire of this activity and leaves the kitchen and the doll sitting in the highchair.

This is a very different play scenario from the actual one. Here, Mario is largely imitating his father's actions and repeating them over and over. There are no new props, new characters or ideas of his own. His play does not change much from beginning to end. It doesn't progress from a more simple beginning in which one action is copied to a more complex phase involving Mario's deep interests and needs. Because of this, Mario's play here is not expressive of the wide range of concerns which are common to children at his stage of development, and he clearly doesn't work on concepts in the way he did in the first scene. He probably doesn't experience the sense of control and mastery that comes from taking charge of play. Thus, many of the benefits to Mario of the play in the first scene do not occur in this second one.

The ideas of the Swiss psychologist, Jean Piaget, help explain why the high-quality play in the first scene is so crucial to the healthy development of young children. Piaget made an important distinction between play and imitation. He saw play as a process where children work on fitting reality to their own inner understanding and needs, where children can take reality and work on it in their own way. This is what Mario was doing when he went from imitating his father to pretending to have a birthday party with his doll and teddy bear. In the course of the play process, as children use their ability to imagine, create and problem-solve, they sometimes change their old ideas and work out new understandings. This is a key source of development and growth in the early years.

For Piaget, imitation is the opposite of play. Imitation involves mainly fitting oneself to reality. When children imitate something, they try to conform to some external model or action, to replicate what they have seen. Imitation can serve a useful role in the development of play. For very young children, who are just beginning to learn that they can perform the same actions they see others performing, imitation can be the first stage of their learning about the power of dramatic play. And older children often effectively use imitation to get started on a new play scene (as when Mario began by copying the actions of his father feeding Rosa in the first scene), or when they first bring to their play a new action they have seen. This can help them expand the repertoire of actions they have available for use in their play.

So, when children play, there is often some external influence that they imitate (such as Mario's father feeding Rosa), but the driving force in play is internal. It is dominated by a child's personal interpretation and transformation of outside events. And whenever something is imitated, it must be transformed through play in order to become meaningful and useful information to a child. So, while imitation can play a useful role in development, a problem can result when children get fixated on it and do not transform what they are imitating into play.

Dramatic Play: An Endangered Species?

The distinction between play and imitation provides a very powerful lens for looking at play. For Piaget, the learning most important to development comes about not by directly copying external ideas or experiences, but by using them in play; to understand anything is to invent it for oneself. It is through this process of transforming reality and developing an understanding of it in play that children invent ideas that are new to themselves. As children play, they try on new roles. They develop their ability to imagine what might be instead of what is. They develop creativity as they combine old elements in new ways and as they devise new possibilities. And problem solving skills are enhanced as children find solutions to the many difficulties they encounter.

Looked at in this way, play not only lends itself to healthy development in children, it can also provide them with the kinds of socially useful skills they will need to solve the problems that lie ahead. And imitation, when it interferes with children's deep involvement in play, can lead to conformity (doing things as they have always been done), and inhibit the development of an individual's full potential. This can have negative effects on the facility with which individuals can adapt constructively to change.

Keeping the distinction between play and imitation in mind can help us decide when children's play is, and is not, of the quality that is likely to best support their full growth and development. It is especially useful for looking at play today because many factors are undermining children's ability to engage in rich dramatic play and are channeling children into imitation.

Children have less time to play. Their lives are often more regimented and scheduled. With more and more two-career families and single parents who work outside the home, children spend more of their time away from home. When they are at school, pressures for "back to basics" often edge play time out of many early childhood classrooms. And, when children finally arrive home for what could be some free-play time, they often land in front of the television set, not in a quiet space playing with their toys or out in the neighborhood playing with friends. Without lots of time, children are less likely to have the opportunity to develop their play.

But this trend has been going on for a long time. That children's play is affected by it is more a side effect of changing patterns of families and schools than it is a direct influence on the nature and meaning of play. And taken by itself, it would not create the concerns we raise throughout this book.

What concerns us now is the direct impact on the very heart of children's play that has resulted from the link-up of television with toys, coupled with profound changes in the nature of the toys (See Chapter Four—"From Sticks and Stones to Lasers"). These changes endanger the play process itself and the mental health and growth of the children who need it. For now, not only do children have less time to play, but when they do play, they are often drawn into imitating what they have seen on TV with toys that tell them how to imitate it. This process—how it occurs, what it means for children and their war play and what adults can do about it—is the subject of the rest of this book.

GUIDE
Helping Play Develop

The challenge here is to ensure that children can become involved in rich and meaningful dramatic play. For dramatic play like Mario's to occur, children need to become deeply involved in their play—almost lost in it. The environment that is available for play and the ways that it gets used will have an important impact on whether this involvement happens. Time, space and materials all can contribute to what children end up doing. Whatever your resources are, you can support your child's play and show that you value it through the environment you create and through careful intervention and facilitation.

◆ **Try to find times and places where your child can play without frequent intrusions.**

One reason children don't get very involved in their play is that they are not sure they can have play time which won't be disrupted. If every time your child starts to take off with her play, an interruption occurs—for example, a younger sibling grabs a toy, a television is turned on or a parent asks her to move her things to make room for dinner—she will quickly learn that it doesn't pay to get very involved in what she is doing. And she may feel that what she is doing isn't very important.

Try to set someplace aside where your child can play. It can be a little corner of a room. It need not be available at all times. But it should belong to the child during the play time. Perhaps after lunch the space under the kitchen table can become a space ship when a sheet is put over it. Or, a couch might be moved out a few feet from a wall and dramatic play items arranged there to create an area for dramatic adventures. And, if you see your child starting to set up his play in an inconvenient place, suggest an alternative location before he gets too far.

One parent made the lower part of the pantry in her apartment into a play space for her three-year-old child away from the crawling sibling. In one drawer she put his favorite dress-up things. On the shelves she put ice cream containers with such things as crayons, scissors, paper and little dinosaurs. The child could go into "his" pantry at will, close the door and "keep the baby out"!

◆ **When an interruption in play is inevitable, try to prepare your child.**

While a goal is to help children keep their constructive play going as long as possible, there will be times when an interruption is unavoidable. When play time is coming to a close, give a warning in advance so your child can wind the play down. If you know an outing to the store is coming, tell the playing child a few minutes in advance so it doesn't come as a surprise. If a younger sibling is about to get up from a nap, help him figure out what he can do to keep the play going—for example, by finding an acceptable role for the sibling in the play, by diverting the sibling with another activity, or by moving the play to a safer location. Such warnings convey to your child that you care about what he is doing and are looking out for his interests.

♦ **Try to help your child know where her play materials are.**

One thing that helped Mario's play develop was the supply of interesting props he could find easily. If children are going to get deeply involved in their play and with their playthings, they need to know what things they have and where to find them. It's easy for a child to get distracted from play while going in search of a certain prop.

Help your child organize and store his play materials. Start out by organizing the playthings with your child. Let her help decide where to keep things. The order that makes sense to you may not make sense to your child. Young children can have a hard time organizing objects into clear categories—for instance, into categories of animals, space things or building things. Follow her lead in deciding what things should be kept with what other things. If she plays an active role she will be more likely to remember where to find what she wants when she wants it.

Keep playthings in labelled containers so they can be easily found and put away again. The empty packages from many food and household items work well—for instance, ice cream or fruit containers, coffee cans with tape put around the top, empty shoe boxes. With masking tape or blank stickers, make simple labels with pictures to identify what is in a container. You can also write a word or two to go with the picture. A young child will quickly learn to "read" the picture labels to find what he wants and as he gets older he may begin to "read" the words.

All of your efforts will make the job of cleaning up much easier too. Your child will know what to put where. Of course, it will not work like magic. You will still need to help, remind, suggest. Allow time at the end of play for clean-up. Give a warning a few minutes beforehand so your child knows it's coming. If a lot of playthings are out, suggest an easy starting point such as, "The cars can go in their container first, then the shells can go in theirs." This can make the job less overwhelming by helping to break it into littler parts.

When arranging your child's toys, you will find unique approaches that work for your child's particular circumstances. For example, five-

Keeping play things in labeled containers can help support children's play.

year-old Miguel and his younger sister and brother kept all their toys together. One day Miguel announced he was going to play "space man" and started going through the communal toy box. He couldn't find anything he needed and ended up having a tantrum. His father helped him to separate out some of the play things that he liked to use in his "space man" play and put them in a box under his bed. Miguel spent hours with this small collection of treasures and always returned them under his bed.

♦ **Observe and learn as much as you can about your child's play.**

As we stress throughout this book, the best way to figure out how to support play is to observe it and learn as much as you can about it. Then you'll be in a better position to decide what will help your child. What you learn will form the basis of whatever you do. When you first look at play, there will be a lot to see. These questions might help:

—What themes seem most important?
—How does the play change over time?
—What kind of variety occurs—with the characters, story and materials?
—How much of the play involves similar themes, scripts and actions?
—Where do the ideas come from—from friends, school, family, television?
—How are his everyday experiences coming into the play?
—Is she making up ideas of her own?

◆ **Try to facilitate the play starting from what the child is doing.**

Play belongs to children. They should be able to design, shape and direct it themselves; ideally adults should not interfere with children's play too much. But today, children may need some help developing and elaborating their play—help in becoming involved, help in moving beyond imitative play.

After observing for a while, you may decide to try some small interventions, especially if you feel the play seems to be overly narrow or stuck in some way. It will be crucial to remember that children should always feel in control of their own play and that you are merely facilitating that process. Your child should always feel he doesn't have to use your suggestion. If it has been made gently, it can be dropped gently by the child, too.

While the play is going on, small interventions which connect to what is happening at that moment work best. They can help to enrich the play without intruding.

Try making an occasional comment about what you see happening. The best comments simply describe what is going on, but don't evaluate it in any way. They are also brief and do not interrupt the flow of play. You might say, "I see that GI Joe and Cobra are fighting again," or "It looks like you found a different way to trap Skeletor." Comments like this can be very useful. They show that you see and appreciate what is happening in the play, and they encourage conversation about it. Sometimes the talk can lead a child to a deeper level of involvement, or a new idea or direction for play.

Another effective technique is to ask open-ended questions. An open-ended question has many possible answers. It lets you provide input without being bossy. Such questions can lead children toward some new idea that they might not have thought of alone. For example, when Mario was feeding his doll, his father might have asked, "Can you make other things for your baby to eat?" or "What will you do with your baby after you feed him?" No one question is ever right or wrong when you attempt this kind of intervention. What works will depend on what you are seeing and your own intuition about what would be an appropriate extension of what is happening at the time.

You can also provide an interesting new play material. Offering something new at the right moment can lead a child in new directions. There is no "right" material to introduce; it depends on what you have available at the moment and whether you think your child will be able to connect it to what he is already doing. In the second imitative scene, Mario's father could have given Mario the kind of things we saw him using in the first play scene—a set of small blocks, or toy animals, or playdough. We can't predict what Mario would have done with them, but they all suggest possibilities without telling Mario how to use them. Open-ended materials like these are especially good at helping to expand play because they can be shaped to fit the child's imagination, ideas and needs. (See Chapter Four—"From Sticks and Stones to Lasers".)

You can also make small suggestions to help your child build onto what he was already doing. In Mario's case, his father might have said, "Maybe you could make a special place for your doll to eat with your blocks," or "Would you like to give your baby a bath after breakfast?"

♦ **Help your child bring many different interests and themes into her play.**

Most children do have topics and roles that are their favorites, and they often play them out over and over again. But it is important for children to be able to incorporate more of their experience into play than with just one or two themes.

Themes with which children have had a lot of direct experience and those which provide dramatic and clearly identifiable actions that can easily be acted out in play offer the greatest possibilities for rich dramatic play.

While familiar daily events in a child's life can seem rather routine to adults, for children they offer endless opportunities for play and learning. Mario used the ordinary event of his father feeding baby Rosa as the "starting point" for a rich and deeply involving play scenario. Such daily experiences as preparing food and eating, dressing and getting ready for bed, drives in the car, the weather and how it effects daily activities all provide rich content for play. So do such concrete things as your home and what's in it, the family members and their roles, and people in the community such as firefighters, shopkeepers, medical workers and mail carriers.

There are also the special events in your child's life which can add important new themes to play—birthday parties, family outings, trips or vacations. And there are the potentially more traumatic experiences—illness or injuries, doctor visits or stays in the hospital, a fire in the neighborhood, getting lost in the supermarket or breaking a special object. These kinds of events are often the ones that children have the most need to play out in order to work out some understanding and resolution of what occurred.

When your child has been playing out a particular theme for a long time without a lot of variation, use one of the techniques described in the last guideline to try to bring in a new topic or role which might be interesting to your child. Pretending to feed baby dolls can lead nicely into cooking for or bathing the dolls. Firefighter or police play can often be guided into hospital play to help the victims. When your child has been involved in a nurturing domestic role for a while, you can help him try a new role like "going to work." With any of the interventions you try, the more direct experience your child has had with what you suggest, the better he will be at using your input in a meaningful way.

♦ Try to give your child as many concrete experiences with everyday activities and objects as you can.

Direct experience in daily activities forms the basis of meaningful play. Sometimes it is too difficult to incorporate a child into daily activities; you just need to get the job done fast. But include him in your activities when you can. Because of "labor saving devices" (such as washing machines and food processors) and changing family patterns, today's children are less a part of the workings of daily life than at any time in history. Many children are getting a narrower and narrower range of direct experiences to use for their play. So now, more than ever before, we need to do special things to make sure they get it. When you do the laundry, involve your child in sorting the clothes, putting them in the washer with the soap, putting in the coins if it's a laundromat. Involve him in a range of daily kitchen tasks—cooking with you, setting the table and cleaning up, putting out the garbage (and watching the garbage truck come).

When you go on errands outside the home, think of them as mini field trips. At the supermarket, doctor's office or post office, point out some of the interesting things you see there. For instance, at the post office take a look at what the post office workers are doing and the equipment they use. Talk about what happens to your package or letter. At the supermarket ask your child to help find the items you need and watch how the shelves are stocked and how the check-out process works.

3
Bang! Bang! You're Dead!
Why War Play?

Many children have a real passion for war play. Once they discover it, it quickly becomes their favorite form of pretend play. Often they engage in it with an intensity and commitment which is not present in their other dramatic play. Parents see this passion in their children and ask where it comes from and where it will lead; they worry that it will contribute to militaristic values in adulthood.

At the same time, a great many of the parents we've talked with, who grew up to have peaceful values, describe their own war play as children. Often, when we talk to a group of adults who are concerned about war play today and ask them how many of them engaged in war play as children, three-quarters of the hands in the audience, those of both men and women, go flying up. And faces usually light up as well, because war play is almost universally remembered by parents of today as a happy part of their childhood experience. These adults realize that children can play at war without necessarily learning to glorify it or wishing to promote it as adults.

War play, when it is rich and elaborated like Mario's doll play, can provide children with the same benefits that all forms of dramatic play can provide. In fact, as a particularly powerful form of pretend play, it offers an arena in which children can feel strong and empowered, and in which they can work on a variety of concepts. In war play, children can work on their understanding of the boundaries between pretend and reality, build basic cognitive concepts, develop a beginning understanding of political and moral ideas, and even learn about cooperation and the needs of others. Further, in a society in which children are exposed to violent images in their environment from an early age, war play can serve as an important vehicle through which children can work on the thoughts and feelings they have about the violence they see around them. We will not argue that if children are not engaged in war play, they need to be encouraged to be; only that, properly managed when it does occur, war play can be a positive force in a child's growth.

Let's look at the war play of Jake and Owen and see what children can gain as they engage in war play of their own making.

Jake and Owen Capture the Romans: "Old-Fashioned" War Play

Jake (four and a half years old) and Owen (just six years old) are having a snack at Jake's kitchen table. Owen holds his banana to his mouth and makes a bunch of unintelligible noises.

Owen: I'm talking in my special army code so the Romans won't hear me. I'm the commander of all the armies. You're the commander of one of my armies, Jake. Calling Sandy's army, calling Sandy's army! (Sandy is Owen's little sister.) Can you hear me? I'm the best, then you Jake, then Sandy's army.

Jake: Girls aren't in the army. They don't like fighting.

Owen: Some like to fight in the army.

Jake: Yes. Like Rachel in my nursery school. She fights.

Owen: We shouldn't fight with Sandy, she's little. No one should fight. Let's only kill the kid monsters so no one has to fight anymore— except when there are wars. (The boys and their friends have invented the "kid monster" who tries to scare and eat children.) Jake, we killed the kid monster at school.

Jake: Is he dead? Will told me that the man and woman kid monsters keep having baby kid monsters—there's always more.

Owen returns to talking into his banana "walkie-talkie" about the Roman army attack. He asks Jake for his cap gun and claw (a long-handled stick with a claw at the end which closes when the handle is squeezed). They run outside swinging the weapons. Jake grabs bushes with the claw while Owen "shoots" at the bush.

Jake: We're *really* killing the kid monster. I hate it. It's the worst monster. Pow! I got it that time.

Owen: No, it's over there. Bang, Bang!

They continue running and making weapons' noises. They grab a bush and start hitting and pulling it with their hands. One of the branches of the bush breaks off. Jake's mother comes out and takes the gun and claw away saying, "You were using these to hurt things, so I'm going to take them for awhile."

Owen: What do you have for weapons now, Jake?

Jake: I don't know. (pause) Oh. I have my Poly-M's upstairs. (Poly-M's are a construction toy with interlocking pieces that come in four colors. The pieces come in units of one, two or three.) Mom, can I have my gun back just to go upstairs? The monsters won't come if I have it.

Jake goes off with the gun and quickly returns with the Poly M's. The two boys begin to build their weapons.

The Poly-M gun Jake made to fight the Romans

Owen: I need five ones.

Jake (counting them out carefully): You can have six so mine has the same on both sides. Can I have your red three's and I'll give you my yellow three's? I need reds for fire. (They trade.)

Owen: Mine is the biggest.

Jake: No, mine's going to be the biggest too. Oh, my gun doesn't have a place for the walkie-talkie. I have to take it apart.

Owen: Mine is going to have a space viewer. (Holds up his creation with a smile.) Do you like my gun?

Jake: Yes. Do you like mine? This is my space viewer.

Owen: You're a good person for an army man, I must say, Jake. This gun doesn't shoot anything but Romans. That's the bullets I put in. They say "Romans." Here, Jake. Take some of my Roman bullets (pretends to hand Jake something).

Jake: Okay. Mine are Roman fire bullets.

Owen: If I touch this blue piece and it's hot, that means a Roman is coming. Then if I shoot he'll be turned into a color.

Jake: Oh, so our bullets can turn the Romans into a color?

Owen: Yes, with their fire. The fire from real bullets can really kill people. But our bullets turn them into colors.

Jake: Can people be turned into colors?

Owen: No. You would vanish and a color would appear where you were and then that color would disappear into heaven. In Star Wars when Darth Vadar killed him, he vanished and all you could see was the color of his coat.

After a half-hour of building they run outside to fight Romans with their completed weapons.

Owen: That one fell down dead. That one fell down dead. That one fell down dead. That one fell down dead.

Jake: And when they fall down dead, I lick them and they turn to stone! Oh, no! Now they're turning me into stone, Owen! I know, I'll be invisible so they can't change me. Then I can go and lick them and then shoot them.

Owen: And when they're dead we can put them into prison and poison them. Then they'll really be dead. (pause) You know, this shoots all the way around the world—from Boston to Boston . . . all the way to China and back to Boston. That's because the world goes round and round.

Jake: The Romans tied me to the ground. Help! Help, Owen!

Two weeks later, Jake gets a library book about the Romans, with many grand pictures of their buildings. When he returns home he insists on telephoning Owen.

Jake: Owen, don't fight the Romans. (pause) You can't. I like their buildings—a lot. I don't want you to fight them. (He listens to Owen, nods, says "okay" and hangs up.)

Jake (to his parents): Me and Owen have a plan to not fight the Romans. We'll just run away from them. We can fight the kid monster but not the Romans!

Why Do They Love It So Much?

Jake and Owen are having a wonderful time as they make weapons and pretend to fight the Romans and the kid monster. Throughout the play they feel very strong and in control as they plan and then carry out their attacks. They are in charge of what happens and they can make sure they always win. They are able to express feelings of hostility toward their imaginary foes, and to gain control of these feelings within themselves. And they are completely engaged and absorbed in their play.

Perhaps more than any other form of dramatic play, war play is appealing because it allows children to feel so powerful. Whatever characters they are pretending to be—superheroes, soldiers, "Masters of the Universe"—this sense of power can be felt in reenacting these roles. At an age when children can feel helpless and out of control as they face such scary tasks as needing to separate from home and go to school or daycare, this sense of having control and power can be very important. It is often children who are experiencing some difficult life event—such as parental divorce or a stay at a hospital—who seem most involved in war play.

Jake and Owen's war play also fits neatly with the way they think. Young children often form simple and unidimensional categories—for good and bad, right and wrong, friend and enemy, girl and boy. Good is good and bad is bad; you can be one but not both. Jake and Owen have divided their play world up this way. They are the "good guys" and the Romans and kid monster are the "bad guys"; once these labels are assigned everyone's role is clear-cut and uncomplicated. When Jake says, "We're really killing the kid monster. I hate it. It's the worst monster," he doesn't need to worry about why its bad. He can just hate it because he has labelled it "bad." The content of war play provides children with many opportunities to use these kinds of easily defined categories.

In addition, war play involves dramatic elements, such as noisy guns, explosions and fast action. This also connects well with how young children think. They are drawn to the concrete and dramatic aspects of things, that which they can easily identify and understand. They do not worry about the logical connections—the logic of how and why things are like they are. We see this as Jake and Owen get totally absorbed in the concrete aspects of building their toy guns with the Poly-M's (for instance, space viewers, walkie-talkies and bullets), and on the many things that their guns can do (such as shoot Romans with fire, and turn people into colors). They do not seem interested in why a bullet can only kill Romans or can turn the Romans into a color.

The Potential Value of War Play

As we have already suggested, war play also has potential value which goes beyond the simple fact of its appeal. Some of these benefits can result from all healthy forms of dramatic play; still others are specific to war play itself. Let's examine these each in turn, using the play of Jake and Owen as examples.

Sorting out fantasy and reality   Jake and Owen are learning many things as they play. Their play is helping them sort out fantasy and reality. For instance, their "bad guys" include imaginary monsters and the Romans, whom they also treat as pretend. But when they find out later that the Romans built lovely buildings, they decide the Romans can no longer be the pretend "bad guy" in their play.

Children frequently experience confusion about where pretend stops and real begins. They constantly bring the pretend from their play back to the real world and what they learn in the real world back to their play. As they do this, they are getting to know and understand the boundary between pretend and real better. For example, when Jake is afraid to go upstairs alone because he's afraid of monsters, he asks his mother for his cap gun. Just recently, he's decided that carrying a weapon (that he uses in play) for protection can help him feel strong against his fears in daily life. Perhaps because of the intense emotional involvement and the powerful images and actions that have to be kept under control, war play more than other forms of play seems to push children to the limits of their understanding about pretend and real. And it provides a forum where they can continually explore and refine their understanding.

"This is me being angry, so angry I stamp my feet when people are visiting me. Mommy yelled at me because I interrupted Michael. I wanted to buy a gun to shoot Mommy but I couldn't drive the car. Except it's just pretend. Mommy didn't buy it for me because she was too busy talking. Mommy put me in my room when I was naughty."
—Sonya, age 4

For young children, the worlds of fantasy and reality often come together in the same experience.

Building basic cognitive concepts Jake and Owen are also working out cognitive concepts as they play. For example, they are using math concepts when they work out how to share the Poly-M's.

They put the building pieces into categories (of color and size), count them, compare sizes of guns and quantities of Poly-M pieces, and subtract and add pieces to their guns. They are developing language skills as they talk about what they do and communicate their ideas to each other.

Developing political and moral ideas Beyond these basic language and math concepts, their play also helps them develop political and moral concepts, including ideas about war and peace. By the very nature of their play, they are using and expanding their understanding of enemies, killing, death, weapons, conflict, conflict resolution, and the nature of good and evil. While what these things mean to them is quite different from adult meanings, what they learn is part of the foundation for adult political thinking.

For example, Jake and Owen's concept of killing and death is revealed many times as they play. Owen says he killed the "kid monster" at school and Jake asks if he's dead. They shoot the kid monster over and over, and keep saying he's really dead. They do the same thing when they kill a Roman and take him to the hospital to poison him and really kill him. And they never think about the implications of their killing—for instance, whether it hurts, or how the family and friends of those killed feel. When they discuss whether the kid monster is really dead, Jake connects it to what he knows about birth—" . . . the man and woman kid monsters keep having baby kid monsters so there are always more." And Owen seems to be trying very hard to grasp the meaning of killing when he says, "No one should fight . . . except when there are wars."

Making sense out of experience These last comments and many others illustrate how Jake and Owen use play to make sense out of the things they have taken in from the world around them—on the news, on violent cartoons, from parents, peers and books. There is really a flow of information between play and concepts about the world rather than a neat compartmentalization between the two. Children learn things about the world, bring those ideas to play, expand on them in play, and take them back to their understanding of the world.

Learning to cooperate and consider other points of view It is often easier to see how children learn about conflict and enemies in war play than to see what they learn about cooperation and the needs of others. Young children's thinking is egocentric. This doesn't have a pejorative meaning; only that they tend to see one perspective on a situation, and it is usually their own. But in this play scene, while Jake and Owen make weapons and carry on battles, they also work hard to take each other's ideas and needs into account. They share and negotiate over materials when they are building with the Poly-M's. They plan actions together when they discuss how to kill the kid monster and the Romans. And they try hard to understand each other, to incorporate one another's ideas into their play—for instance, Owen says, "Then if I shoot, the Roman will be turned into a color," and Jake responds, "Oh, so our bullets can turn the Romans into a color?" All of these examples show how in war play, as well as in other forms of social play, children help each other's ideas to grow and change.

Working on individual interests and needs   Even as Jake and Owen cooperate and work together so successfully as a team, there are many ways we can see their own individual ideas, interests and needs expressed. Owen seems concerned with how what he knows about the real world fits into what is happening in his play. As a result, he often has a hard time staying absorbed in his world of pretend for very long. For instance, early on when he suggests that "they only kill the kid monster so that no one has to fight anymore . . . except when there are wars," he is connecting real wars with their play killing. He does this again later on when the boys are making their guns. He says that bullets can turn Romans into a color with their fire and then adds that the fire from real bullets can really kill people. And at the end when the boys are "fighting the Romans," Owen once again brings in his knowledge of the real world when he stops and begins a monologue about how his gun shoots all the way around the world, and then begins explaining that the world goes round and round.

Jake, on the other hand, seems quite content to keep his fantasy world separate from what he knows about the real world. While he does bring ideas from play into daily life and vice versa, he does not seem to be worried about making the logical connections between fantasy and reality. And it is interesting that Jake rarely responds to Owen's monologues about how things are in the world; he usually picks up on something else that Owen has said that is within their game of fantasy. For example, it is the fight with the Romans and whether bullets can turn people to colors that interests Jake, not whether bullets can really kill people.

War Play Changes with Age

Jake is four and a half years old and Owen is six. While we have looked at how many of the underlying issues in their war play cut across age and stage differences, some of what Jake and Owen do is related to this difference. And while for the most part we do not use the "age and stage" approach in this book, knowing the basic progression of war play as it develops over a period of years can be very helpful to the parent who is trying to understand this play.

There are many issues in human development, including play, that follow understandable and predictable progressions. Knowing what to expect at a certain age can serve to reassure parents that what their children are doing is within the range of what is considered "normal." It can also provide a lens for recognizing the key developmental milestones that are likely to occur and how to nurture them. But when reading about the ages and stages described here, remember that age norms cannot replace our appreciation for the unique qualities of the play of any one child.

The birth of war play   Before children can become involved in war play, they must learn to pretend. They must learn that one object can stand for another object, and that a pretend action can represent a real action. Usually, children begin to enter the world of pretend with objects. A block becomes a "cup" which the child pretends to drink from or a scarf becomes a hat that is placed on the head. Children also learn that they themselves can pretend do be someone else and imitate his or her actions. Children will pretend to be a parent and feed a baby, just as their parents have fed them. Through this healthy imitation, pretend or symbolic play is born and children will gradually learn a wider repertoire of pretend behaviors that grow out of this initial symbolic imitation. It is also how they begin to learn to use their pretend play to help them understand their experience.

These basic tools of pretending have become a regular part of most children's repertoire before they are three years old. At this early phase, they are usually working on these skills with objects, people and actions that are most familiar and central to their lives. But once children have these tools at their disposal, they are ready to try out war play. They can take a stick, turn it into a gun and pretend to shoot. They will do this after they have seen other, usually older, children's gun play, or after they've had some other exposure to "shooting." They may soon also begin to imitate other actions they see older children doing in their war play such as falling down "dead." They will do these things without much awareness of what real guns are or what killing and death really mean.

Had Sandy, Owen's three-year-old sister, been involved in Jake and Owen's play, her play would have been quite different from theirs. She might have picked up a few Poly-M's that were randomly connected together and pretended to shoot. She might have run around imitating the boys' actions and sound effects—shooting, falling down dead and going "Pow, Bang!" She would probably have responded to direct commands from the boys about what to do—where to go, when to shoot, when to fall down and get up. And if one of them had pointed a gun at her and said, "Pow! You're dead!" she probably would have started to cry. But the specific content of Jake and Owen's play and their discussion about it would have been lost to Sandy, who would focus on acting out the visible actions. The specific attributes of the

Poly-M weapons, who the enemies were, and whether or not they died would have had little meaning to her.

War play scenarios and social play begin   Usually between the ages of three and four years, children's growing ability to pretend leads them to act out their own little themes. At four, Jake has gotten very good at this, especially with Owen's help. During this phase, children bring in information they have learned from sources external to themselves, such as television. They try out being specific characters whose attributes they spell out. Their scenarios often follow definite sequences which begin to have starting points and conclusions. As they develop this kind of play, playmates become increasingly important. Children begin to plan together, assign roles to each other and act out the plans together. This doesn't mean they stick to their plans. As they get involved in the play the excitement of the action often leads to new ideas and actions.

It is often hard for an adult to see how the pieces in the play connect at this stage. The pieces follow a logic of their own and children are not bothered by this. They focus on what they are doing at a given moment, not on how they got there or where they will go afterwards; their play is like a series of static slides rather than a movie. They don't often worry much about what they can't see and do—why some guys are good and others are bad, what happens to the bad guy once he is shot, how they managed to get from earth to space. And because of this single focus, children this age can get completely lost in the world of pretend, rarely thinking about the connections between their play and the real world. Often they get so involved in what they are doing that they lose control and become hurtful, or they forget about their playmates and go about doing their own separate things side by side.

The whole scene becomes important   As children approach six or seven years, a major transition in how they think begins to occur which has powerful effects on their play. They move toward a more dynamic way of thinking, in which several ideas begin to be interconnected and related to a larger whole. As a result, planning becomes important and plans are actually carried out in play. The play begins to follow a logic more understandable to adults. One action often leads to a logical next action. Logical reasons for what happens in the play are worked out—how the weapons will accomplish their task, why the bad guys are bad. Playmates usually stick to the same plot and adjust their actions to fit into the play. And it becomes increasingly difficult for children this age to keep the pretend world and real world separate. These changes are also reflected in the battle scenes that children draw, and for many children, battle scenes become as satisfying as war play.

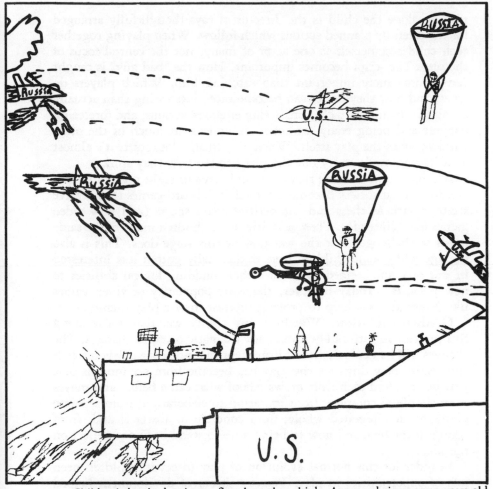

Children's battle drawings reflect how they think. At around six or seven years old the whole scene becomes important.

Owen is in the midst of this transition. His ability to plan, coordinate actions and construct a logic for the play provides much of the focus and direction for what happens. He is also the one for whom the realities of the world constantly intrude. In a deep sense, as Owen plays we can see him losing his innocence. He is reaching a level of logical thinking where he will soon be unable to suspend himself totally in the world of pretend war.

Rules, strategy and planning prevail   By the time children reach seven or eight years, their new abilities to think about several things at a time, use logical causality, see all the parts within a whole, and imagine what they can't see all contribute to major shifts in their play. Increasingly it becomes like a staged dramatic production. When playing alone the child is the director of toys thoughtfully arranged for the carefully planned actions which follow. When playing together each child sees herself as one actor of many, not the central focus of the play. The script becomes important. How the "bad guy" is caught can become more important than catching him. Which players do what, and how they do it, can become more interesting than actually doing it. Planning attacks, predicting enemies' actions, and foreseeing dangers and being ready for them are at least as much of the older child's play as the play itself. When play finally does start, it's almost as if its purpose is to try out the plans to see how they work.

It is interesting to note that at around seven or eight years old many children in our society become involved with board games that involve strategy such as chess and competitive team sports (and now video games like Nintendo). These activities offer children many of the same kinds of challenges that the war play at this stage does. This is also the age when some children have traditionally gotten less interested in war play and seemed to transfer their budding logical abilities to new pursuits. (Today however, the wide popularity of video games like Nintendo may help to prolong interest in war play themes.)

Gradual evolution   Watching any child's war play move along this impressive path rarely reveals any dramatic or rapid changes. The changes will be gradual, almost imperceptible, until one day you watch and realize how different the play has become from six months or a year before. And each shift grows out of what came before and moves from simple to complex; from imitation to elaboration; from separate pieces to an integrated whole; from concrete to abstract; and, from acting in the here and now to being able to stand back and reflect on the play.

In order for this normal evolution of play to occur, children need lots of opportunities to play. Piaget's theory of development helped explain why. As children play using their current best understanding of the world, they can encounter ideas, situations and information which do not quite match their current views. A feeling of confusion or disequilibrium can result. As children try to sort out this confusion they often change their old ideas to take into account the new. Growth in thinking results.

When children play at war, one way their attitudes and ideas develop is through experiencing disequilibrium so it can be valuable to find ways to encourage it. One important way it is created during play is through interactions with other children who invariably have different ideas. We see this happening with Jake and Owen. For instance, early in their play Jake says that girls do not like to fight and do not serve in the army. Owen contradicts Jake's idea and tells him that girls do in fact serve in the army. Jake listens to Owen and then tries to think of a girl whom he knows who does fight. What has happened, in effect, is that Owen has helped Jake break down a stereotyped idea he held about girls.

There are also other sources of disequilibrium—parents, teachers, some chance exposure to information which contradicts, by just a little bit, some concept that has already been worked out in play. War play is unique to each individual, it changes moment by moment; what is of interest today may be put on the back burner tomorrow. And because disequilibrium originates within the child, what will create it isn't easy to predict.

All War Play Is Not the Same

When children engage in war play that has the creative and dynamic qualities observed here in the play of Jake and Owen, and when it evolves and advances in the ways described above, then there is the potential for a tremendous amount of growth and learning. In war play such as this, children are working on their own ideas and are in charge of what happens. Through this play they can develop cognitive concepts such as mathematical ideas; they can develop many early political concepts and values and learn about positive social relationships; and, they can gain a sense of mastery as they use play to integrate and understand their experiences. And they work on these things as individuals, using their imagination and creativity in their own unique ways.

But, children's war play can be of different quality, and we see this with Jake and Owen. What if their play had stayed like it was near the beginning when they were attacking the bushes with the play claw and cap gun? In this section they got very violent. Their early childhood egocentrism and the tendency to get consumed by one idea or action took over. They seemed to be involved in violence for its own sake, to the exclusion of anything else. If their play had been only this, they would not have been experiencing the rich range of ideas that we see once Jake's mother takes away the gun and claw and they have to make their own weapons with Poly-M's.

Most of Jake and Owen's play is constructive, elaborate dramatic play that furthers their development in many ways. But war play like that with the cap gun and claw is of dubious value. Its focus is on being violent; it has the narrow focus of imitative play that is talked about throughout this book. For some children today, this kind of war play takes up much of their play time. When the quality of war play declines and the quantity increases then there is cause for concern about the lessons children are learning as they play. (See Chapter Seven—"Learning About War; Learning About Peace.")

So when children engage in war play, the important questions have to do with the quality of that play. How much of it is theirs? How much of it is written and directed by the children themselves? How many of the issues in the play are their issues? How many of the questions are their questions? How does the play develop and change over time, and what values are being served by it?

Today Children Aren't Calling the Shots

Some adults, who have a gnawing feeling that something is wrong now, find the fact that they turned out all right in spite of their war play a source of reassurance. They should not feel reassured.

While old-fashioned war play can be extremely valuable, as we shall see in the next chapter, war play today is often not like the war play that we engaged in as children. Many of the ideas do not come from the children's own minds nor are they expressive of children's individual needs in the way they were for Jake and Owen. They come from television programs and toys, and they come from the people who make them. Today, when children play with GI Joe and Sergeant Slaughter, it's hard for them to bring in their own ideas or to achieve the quality of war play that Jake and Owen showed. It is difficult for children growing up now to use their war play for their own self-defined ends. More often they use it to imitate the violence they have seen and this is what makes today's breed of war play so worrisome.

We need to figure out a way to deal with this problem, but it is not easy. It's tempting to say, let's just do whatever it takes to stop our children's war play. We wish we could advise parents to do this. But as we argued in Chapter One, banning war play is not usually a viable option.

GUIDE
Guiding War Play

We suggest that parents can help children move from imitative war play to a kind which will help them grow and master their experience: war play in which children themselves are calling the shots. We empathize with the many adults who find it hard to watch their children's war play too closely, much less get involved with it. Many of us experience ambivalence when we see children "fighting and killing," even if it's "only pretend" and even if we try to keep in mind that it has different meaning for children than it does for us. And unlike doll or house play or play with other themes, we share little common experience with our children's war play. But by watching closely, we can find ways to take informed and active roles in guiding it toward its greatest developmental effectiveness.

♦ **Know the "scene."**

Know what is influencing your child's war play. What television programs does he watch at home or at friends' homes? What are the programs about? What does he include in his play that is learned from television or friends? What toys are the current favorites with your child and his peers?

It is often difficult to figure out what is going on in a child's play—who the characters are, what the action is all about, what the action connotes for the child—without knowing something about the popular culture he is in. Even children who aren't often in toy stores and who don't watch a lot of TV are aware of what's important in their culture. Because the TV shows and toys are changing so fast, keeping track of the latest trends can be a constant job.

You can do this by watching the popular television shows (either with your child or on your own if your child doesn't watch them) so you know about the themes and characters. Looking over toys at playmates' houses and in toy stores, and reading the descriptions on toy packages will also help you know what your child and his friends are into.

One parent, whose four-year-old son loved playing with toy dinosaurs, was suddenly puzzled when she saw his play change. He began to tape "weapons" made of little sticks onto his dinosaurs and to orchestrate violent battles among them. Only when she visited a toy store did she understand the change. Prominently displayed was a whole new line of "good and evil dinosaurs," each heavily armed with a weapon. Evidently, his friends at school were much more aware of the new trends than her son, but he was quickly catching up!

♦ **Find out how involved your child is in war play.**

How much of his total play time involves war play? What other kinds of play and play themes interest your child? Do different kinds of play occur over a few days or a week or do war play themes dominate?

The amount of time a child spends on war play, and the range of activities which occur in the course of several play sessions can tell you a lot about where and how you might begin to take a role. A child who spends most of his time with war play themes might need help branching off and finding other compelling ideas to use in his play. A child who flits from topic to topic may benefit most from being helped to get more deeply involved in his play and sustaining it over longer periods. Many children choose a play theme and stay involved with it for several days before moving on to a new area, so you need to observe over a period of time to get a realistic picture here.

◆ **Think about imitation and play.**

How much does your child repeat similar scripts and actions? What kind of variety occurs in the characters involved, the story, and materials? Does your child bring in his own ideas that do not come directly from television? Are some aspects of his war play more original or less original than others?

As we argue throughout this book, one of the biggest worries about war play today is that the television/toy link-up and its focus on violence in war play threatens to undermine the whole nature and utility of war play for children. Your answers to these questions will help you decide how well your child's war play is serving his development. Put another way, they will help you determine the degree to which your child is falling victim to the current forces. If you find there is cause for concern, you will want to help your child get more control over his own play. The suggestions in the last chapter for facilitating dramatic play, in general, will help you with the task. In addition, here are ideas that have to do more specifically with war play.

◆ **Support the themes of greatest interest.**

What themes interest your child most? Are they about bad guys, killing, outer space? Do the same themes dominate or do they change from time to time? Where do the ideas come from—television, peers, the child's own experiences and imagination? Is the war play primarily about violence and fighting or are there also nonviolent themes and characters which enter in?

Books, both fiction and nonfiction, can provide more information and ideas about the themes your child finds interesting. They can give children ideas for new actions and props to use in their play. Content from books offers advantages over what children get from television. With television all of the visual images are provided; with books, even with illustrations, words are most important and it is up to children to create their own images to go along with the story. Thus, books leave more room for a child to decide how to use the story in play. In addition, with books you can stop whenever you want to talk about what is happening, imagine what will happen next, decide what else could have happened—all of which will help children develop their ideas and play still further. The final section of this book gives specific suggestions of ways to use books to facilitate play and a few beginning book ideas.

In addition to books, many communities have museums and other public exhibits which can help your child get ideas for developing a play theme further. If you can visit displays about space, sharks, dinosaurs or knights' armour, what he sees and learns will often get worked into his play.

♦ **Try to learn more about the pressing needs and issues being worked on in play.**

Does your child try to focus on being powerful and strong when he plays? Does he put a lot of energy into controlling the people and things around him? Are there particular fears or insecurities he is bringing in such as getting lost, losing his family, fears of monsters, something scary he has seen? What is he trying to sort out through his play—good from bad, right from wrong? How does he separate what is real from what is not? Does he easily forget he is pretending and actually hurt other people?

War play can reveal a lot about your child's developmental needs and how he is feeling. If he is constantly taking the role of the bullying boss with his toys, he may feel a need for more control in his "real" life. In times of stress his war play may be especially revealing. Parents who are in the process of getting a divorce have commented that their children seem to use their war play to express fears, anger and the need to be strong and in contol with new levels of intensity. Children who have had a recent injury or hospitalization often do the same.

Of course, it is important to be cautious about your conclusions and continually reevaluate them. In the earlier example of the child whose dinosaur play suddenly turned violent, his mother initially thought something must have happened that he needed to express in play. While this could still have been a part of what was going on, as we saw, it wasn't the whole picture.

♦ **Keep the age of your child and level of his play in mind.**

Understanding something about ages and stages helps us to appreciate children's play, know how to talk to them about it, and how to intervene appropriately. To some extent, the appropriateness of everything you try will depend in part on the child's age and stage.

In their fight with the Romans, Jake, Owen, and Owen's sister, Sandy, are all at different developmental levels. Partly because of this, each child will use materials, make guns, and pretend about enemies in different ways. If three-year-old Sandy were to make a gun, it would be with two or three Poly-M's fit together. What would be important to Sandy would be the idea that the Poly-M's stood for a gun, and the activity of running around using it. We would not expect Sandy to get involved in making guns with complicated details like the guns of Jake and Owen. If we were to help her with her gun, we would focus on how the Poly-M's fit together and how she was using the gun in play. If we talked about "space viewers" and "Roman fire bullets," Sandy would be very confused.

Likewise, we would not expect Owen to need a cap gun in order to go upstairs (as protection against monsters), but we are not surprised to see Jake do it. We can understand that Jake confuses fantasy with reality at his stage of development, that his imaginary fears are still quite real to him, and that he can ward them off with a cap gun. In trying to help Jake, his mother gives him the gun. She understands that at his stage, the gun does offer Jake the protection he needs.

It would be inappropriate to expect Sandy to understand the complicated idea of enemy that Jake and Owen are evolving, or to expect Jake to remember that people die from real killing while he pretends to shoot. Ages and stages always play an important role in providing us with a framework within which we can understand the behavior of any one child and from which we can plan our own actions.

◆ **Help your child bring familiar everyday experiences into his war play.**

When the content in your child's war play is coming primarily from television-type scripts (and he doesn't have to watch a lot of television for this to happen), he may have a hard time connecting his play with his direct experience and the things he cares about most in everyday life.

Giving your child a few simple toys and props which suggest some of his more common or meaningful experiences can help him bring the experience into war play. Items to use for food such as empty food boxes, plastic food and playdough can suggest connections. So can rubber tubing to use as a pretend fire hose or an old blanket for pretending to go to sleep after the fighting. (See Part II for more suggestions.)

◆ **Support any original play ideas that your child has.**

If children feel that their own inventions are important, it will give them encouragement to try out their own ideas more and more. There are a variety of ways you can convey this sense of appreciation. They are not all easy. Sometimes children's ideas can create an inconvenience or mess and you may need to draw the line.

One day, a child who frequently played with guns found a ball of string and began making a trap to catch the bad guys by stringing it around furniture in the living room. His father, while ambivalent about having a trap in the family's main living area, offered to knot the string ends to the furniture so the trap would work the way the child wanted it. He reluctantly decided that it was real progress for his son's play to shift from guns to traps, and the benefits were worth the inconvenience. He also agreed to let his son keep the string for future "traps" if they cleaned it up together each time.

♦ **Try to help your child keep the lid on his war play.**

You may have found that war play gets out of control more easily than other kinds of play. It can be time-consuming and stressful trying to keep the lid on the play; sometimes you have to maintain almost a constant vigil over it. It can be upsetting to see your child lose control; you've worked hard to help him develop positive social skills and want him to use them.

Children get so intensely involved in war play, and the content they are using is so dramatic and connected to their inner psyche, that they often lose the control they are able to maintain in other situations. Sometimes children forget they are pretending and physically harm something or someone. Sometimes they get so involved in the action that they lose sight of how their playmates are feeling—the effects of their actions on others. They can get so carried away that they forget all norms that have been established for decent play. And when violence is the main focus of children's actions, loss of control is even more likely because this is the most intense and volatile part of war play.

It can be very upsetting to children to lose control of themselves and their behavior. Their growing sense of independence and personal competence can disappear in a flash, leaving them feeling helpless and vulnerable. Children feel best and safest when they know what the limits of a situation are and can keep within them. So for your child's sense of well-being as well as your own, it's vital that you work together to keep war play under control.

♦ **Try to understand what gets the play into trouble.**

Identifying the trouble spots and danger signs is a good place to start figuring out where your help is needed. The following questions might help you do this:

—Are there particular toys or themes that often end up with your child out of control, hurt or angry?

—Are there any warning signs that indicate that the tensions are escalating—things getting louder, more aggressive, quicker paced?

—Are there particular circumstances which make a crisis more likely—when your child is hungry or sleepy, has just had a large dose of television, seems to be bored, plays with a certain friend?

—Are there particular aspects of the play which upset you or cause you to become short-tempered—high volume, getting shot at, running around the house, toys strewn all over?

◆ **Establish an open climate for working on rules and limits together.**

Helping your child develop inner control over his war play should be the main goal of anything you do. You will want to try to create rules and limits that work even when you are not there to enforce them. You don't want to have your child falling apart or sneaking around breaking rules every time you turn your back.

A joint problem-solving approach can help your child develop inner resources. It involves creating a climate which says: "We're in this together and I'll take the lead in helping you work out a solution." You form an alliance with your child for solving problems together. Children feel that the issues that come up in their play are the subject of legitimate discussion and that their input is valued. And when children know they are an important part of the decisons that are made they feel invested in sticking to them. They also learn that they have the power and skill to keep the play under control themselves, but you're there to provide help if it's needed.

There is no simple set of rules for creating this kind of climate. It will take time for your child to learn how to participate actively and effectively in the process. It won't always work as you would like and sometimes your child will take the solutions in some unexpected directions. When it works effectively, you'll know it! Here is an example of a parent's efforts to initiate a conversation with her four-year-old son about problems that arose in his war play.

> **Faye:** Josh, I know how much you love your gun. But every time you play with it, you end up crying. That gun isn't a good plaything for you right now. I don't want to take it away but we need to figure out what to do.
> **Josh:** It's my "He-Man" T-shirt. Whenever I wear it this gun is bad! Put it away. (He starts taking his T-shirt off.)
> **Faye:** Well, let's try it and see if it helps because all this trouble needs to stop.

Obviously, Faye didn't think that the T-shirt was the problem and she never would have suggested this solution herself. But she succeeded in involving Josh in seeing the problem and in finding a solution he is committed to trying. She made it clear they had to come up with a solution (or she would take the gun) but gave Josh the room to develop his own logic rather than imposing her own. Often a child's reasoning makes more sense to him than adults', and therefore is more likely to work. And Faye knew that she and Josh could evaluate his "theory" about the T-shirt later, and try out another solution, if the problem continued. The process of coming up with a solution was at least as important here as the actual solution.

Faye could have used a more authoritarian approach—for instance, simply banning the gun or banishing Josh to his bedroom until he gained control. But it wouldn't have helped him take responsibility for his actions or to think about what he can do next time when a similar problem arises.

♦ **Whenever possible, see the problem coming and try to avoid it.**

This isn't always easy or possible, but if you've learned the danger signs in your child's war play you will sometimes recognize trouble coming. When you see it, think if it's possible to do so in a way that won't bring the play to a halt.

You can try small distractions such as, "Maybe you could make guns with Legos instead of using these cap guns." When distractions work they have the advantage of avoiding the problem while sustaining the play. Redirecting the play by saying, "Let's get out the playdough instead of playing GI Joe," also can work. But it has a bigger impact on altering the play.

There are also approaches which deal more directly with what's happening. They can help children build up a repertoire of skills to use to manage their war play.

You can point out the problem—"It looks like you're having trouble trying to share one gun. If this continues there may be a fight." Often, young chldren are so involved in their play of the moment that they can't imagine in advance where their behavior might lead. They also don't always make logical causal connections between what they're doing now and the possible effects later.

You can plan a solution with your child: "What can you do so you can hunt the 'bad guys' together? . . . Okay, I'll tell you when five minutes are up so you can take turns." It can be difficult for children, who think about one thing at a time, to consider a range of possible solutions so you may have to suggest one or two. The solution they decide on might not always seem like the best one to you, but give them a chance to try it out.

You can also point out what the consequences will be if the problem spot continues: "If that doesn't work, you'll have to put the gun away and you can both use your fingers for guns." Children feel safer when they know, in advance, the limits beyond which they cannot go and what the consequences will be if they exceed them.

◆ **Act quickly when conflicts arise.**

Children need to know that you are there to keep them safe and help them gain control of their behavior when they can't do it themselves. So, when the approaches just discussed above fail and children lose control, your first job is to ensure the safety of everyone.

Every once in a while, removing a child or providing physical restraint is the only way out. An accompanying comment like, "I need to stop you. I can't let you or anyone else get hurt," explains your actions without blaming anyone. Assigning blame isn't very useful when a child is out of control, and furthermore, children rarely lose control on purpose. They lose control because in that particular situation, they didn't have the skills to keep themselves together.

When everyone involved has calmed down, help them share their ideas about what happened. They won't always agree; the way young children think can make agreement hard to achieve. And you may never get the full and accurate story. But by reflecting back what they say, you can help them to decenter, that is, help them hear one another's point of view and try to understand it. "Billy, when you took Howie's "He-Man" and wouldn't give it back, he got very angry and hit you. But Howie, Billy says he waited a long time for a turn and you wouldn't share." Comments like this do not require that the children agree on what happened. They also don't involve you in making value judgments about who is at fault.

Once you have talked about what happened, you will need to decide how to proceed. There will be many times when you think the children are ready to work out a solution together. But, if you think you should stop the play altogether, do it with a comment like, "It's time for you to play separately for awhile, so let's find something each of you can do alone."

◆ **When you have to become involved, try to avoid expressing strong value judgments about the play.**

If you enter in when two children are smashing their action figures into things and shouting, "You're dead!" an instinctive comment might be, "Don't play like that. Stop killing. You shouldn't even pretend to kill." Comments like this won't stop the behavior for long. A descriptive comment like, "There is a serious battle going on here but it's time to end it. What can you do to get out of this hard situation?" is much more likely to foster problem-solving and get their play beyond the violence of the moment. There are other times when it can be more appropriate to discuss your own values about war play with your child. (See the suggestions in Chapter Seven—"War and Peace.")

4
From Sticks and Stones to Lasers
Play with War Toys

As we demonstrated in the last chapter, war play can serve an important developmental function for young children. It can help children as they strive to develop a sense of their own independence, power and strength. It is also well-suited to help them work through their thoughts and feelings about the violence they see around them. Of course we wish, like many parents, that children were not subject to the bombardment of these images as well as the violent reality which seems to be part of contemporary life, and hope all concerned adults will work to change that reality. But, given the world in which children are growing up today, we have argued that banning war play is not only unlikely to be viable in most cases, it is not even likely to be desirable.

Toys as Tools

As we will try to demonstrate in this chapter, however, we are not so sanguine about the contemporary generation of war toys. It's obvious, as any watchful parent knows, that toys influence the play of which they are a part. They are tools for dramatic play which can help a child work on issues he needs to work on. The tools we provide for a child in the form of toys can, as we shall see, be a force for positive development or they can inhibit the kind of creative play necessary for a child's growth.

Many parents express confusion and discomfort in dealing with today's war toys. We believe that's at least in part due to the fact that the new war toys, whole lines of violent and realistic toys modeled after television shows, are not only marketed differently (as we shall see in the next chapter), but are in and of themselves qualitatively different from the war toys parents may themselves have played with as children. To understand these differences and how they exert differing influences over children's play, let's look at James, Henrietta and Calvin as they play with different kinds of toy weapons.

All War Toys Are Not the Same

James

Three year old James is outside playing with toy dinosaurs when he finds a long thin cardboard tube. He points it at nothing in particular, makes shooting noises and shouts, "I'm shooting dinosaurs." He picks up a small rock and asks his mother to tape it onto the end of the tube. Shooting the tube at a toy dinosaur, he says, "Now I can really kill the dinosaurs." Soon he cries out, "Oh, no! I killed a good one by mistake. I'm the doctor. Here, chew on this." He holds the cardboard tube to a toy dinosaur's mouth. "Here now you're better. You can help me kill the bad dinosaurs." He runs off shooting with the tube and carrying the plastic toy animal.

Henrietta

Henrietta is outside squirting everything in sight with the "rifle" water gun she just received for her fourth birthday. "I shot the house. Now I got the tree. Ha, ha, I got you, Dad! I'm good at hitting things. The water really hurts." She hides behind some bushes and shoots at cars that go by (she can't really get the water to go that far). When the water gun is empty, she asks her father to refill it. As she waits she gets a plastic doll. With the refilled gun, Henrietta begins squirting the doll with an accompanying, "Pow, pow! I'm giving you a bath. Now you're all clean. Pow, pow!"

Calvin

Calvin, aged three and a half, is playing with his older brother's Rambo gun. It looks like a "real" rifle and when he pulls the trigger it makes a popping noise and a plastic blade attached to a string flies out. Over and over he pushes the blade into the gun, takes aim, pulls the trigger, watches the blade pop out and grins. His brother comes into the room. Calvin points the gun at him, pulls the trigger and hits him in the leg with the blade as he yells, "I'm Rambo." His brother roughly grabs the gun and runs out of the room, yelling to his mother about what Calvin did. Calvin begins to cry.

James sees all kinds of possibilities for play with the little treasure he's found. The shape of the tube makes him think of a gun (he's probably seen an older sibling or friend with a gun, or seen one on television) and this is how he decides to use it. He demonstrates that he doesn't understand the meaning of killing which he's also picked up elsewhere: to him, it is simply an expression of power not unlike the power of the doctor in dispensing medicine. When he has his mother tape the rock to the end of the tube he is developing his own idea of what a gun is and how it looks. Then, as he creates his little fighting scene, he can change how it is used to fit in with the changes that *he* wants to make in his play. The tube can easily become a doctor's instrument and medicine, and then become a gun again. The tube is an open-ended toy—it does not define for James how it should be used and it can be used in many different ways. He can decide what it is and how to use it. He is in control of his toy.

Based on its similarity to guns she has seen elsewhere (on TV, in a book, in the hands of an older sibling), Henrietta's toy water gun tells her that it is for shooting and this is how she uses it for most of her play. Because it shoots water, it further directs her play to target practice. But, as her attention turns to her doll, she is able to invent another way to use the gun, to give her dirty doll a "bath." While she can't totally forget she is using a gun as she bathes her doll (it's not the gentle bath than most babies get!), the water in the gun seems to help her break away from concentrating only on shooting and helps her to bring other ideas into play. Henrietta strikes a balance here between the gun and herself in controlling the play.

Calvin's Rambo rifle tells him what to do and he can't seem to resist its powerful message. His actions are at first repetitive and then aggressive. The gun and what he knows about Rambo from other sources take over his play so completely that fantasy and reality get jumbled up; pretending to be Rambo he gleefully shoots his brother for no apparent reason. It's almost as if the toy, by its very nature, makes him lose control and hurt his brother. Calvin's "play" remains limited; he doesn't get beyond what the toy defines. He brings little of himself in to shape the scene. Here, *the toy is in control.*

All three of these children seem to love the idea of shooting with their play objects. The sense of power and strength that the toys suggest, at least in part, by how they look, seems to be irresistible to them. Even James' tube, which he ultimately uses in a variety of ways, is first seen and used for the most powerful function it suggests to him given his previous experience.

Just as war play is appealing to many young children because of the opportunity it provides for them to feel strong and in control, so do war toys exert this pull. Because young children are drawn to the most salient aspects of objects, if a toy suggests the possibility of power and violence, then children are likely to use it for that purpose. This is one reason why so many children seem to be seduced so easily by war toys. And once they are seduced into playing a certain way with a toy, the difficulty they have thinking about more than one thing at a time can make it very hard for them to see what else they can do. While these issues apply to all kinds of war toys, we saw with the three toys above that the more highly defined the violent purpose of the toy, the harder it is for the child to get beyond this single use.

In the 1960s, the managing director of Lone Star Products, a manufacturer of children's guns and cowboy equipment pointed out the dangers of highly realistic reproductions of guns because he felt they could inhibit creativity. Calvin, Henrietta and James' play with their "guns" lends credence to this argument. While all three are involved in pretend fighting, James' simple tube allows for the most imagination, while Calvin's elaborate Rambo gun permits the least. James, more than the other two, also gets the greatest benefit from engaging in meaningful dramatic play.

The Phases of Play and the Toy Continuum

When a child gets a new toy she will usually start out by exploring what it can do. With playdough, she might pound, squeeze and poke it; a "He-Man" action figure might have its limbs moved in every possible direction; a gun will be used for shooting. This kind of exploration is a natural way to begin with any play object. Before a child can really play with a toy she needs to know what it can do. But exploration is only one part of using a toy. Sooner or later, a child begins to bring in her own ideas, experiences and questions. Playdough might be rolled into strips and balls and then a story told about a snake eating apples; "He-Man" might have a fight and then be hugged and put to bed because "he's tired after the battle." This is the kind of play we would expect children to be engaged in during most of their play time with toys.

There are several reasons why a child might appropriately stay at the exploratory phase of play with a toy for a long time. Very young children, because they have so much to learn about objects and how they work, might spend much of their play time exploring their toys. And a new toy which is very novel might keep even an older child interested in the early phase for a long time too. In both of these cases, the extended exploration seems understandable and is probably serving a child's needs well.

But, there are also factors which can keep children stuck in this early phase. For instance, with very purpose-specific toys, or a constant barrage of new toys, there is a danger that a child will find it harder to move to the second phase where toys are used in more individual and creative ways.

James, Henrietta and Calvin each has a gun and each clearly loves shooting with it. But, there are striking differences in how their guns influence the play process. James' tube helps him quickly get beyond the exploratory phase to a point where he is acting out his ideas. Henrietta's water gun tells her to shoot and keeps her there for a while, but still leaves room for her to begin to move to more creative play. But Calvin gets stuck in the early phase of toy use; the rifle doesn't let him get beyond imitating Rambo.

You can think of these three guns as falling along a continuum. At one end are open-ended and less structured toys and play materials like James' cardboard tube, playdough, blocks and Legos. They suggest possibilities for play to a child but they can also be used in many different ways. They help children get to the creative play phase. At the other end are toys which are highly realistic and have a single purpose. They tell children how to use them and it's hard to move beyond that specific use. Single-purpose toys tend to keep children at the exploratory phase. Toys like Calvin's Rambo gun and action figures which perform one specific action fall at this end of the continuum.

Somewhere in between these two extremes are toys like Henrietta's water gun, nonspecific action figures and the more recent Lego kits which come with directions for how to build a specific toy. They convey a specific use but leave some room for the child to change it. This kind of toy, when it suggests something familiar—pretend food or a toy telephone or firehat—can help young children get started on a theme and can actually promote creative play.

Open-ended toys are better for children. This is especially true with war toys where single-purpose war toys can keep children focused on violence and aggression. But the history of war toys seems to follow a route which channels children more and more into specific kinds of war play and from toys at the open end of the continuum to the realistic and highly structured end. We only need to look at a few of the milestones in the western history of war toys to see this process occurring.

Changes in Toys; Changes in Play

Until the Industrial Revolution, handmade war toys were only in the hands of the male children of nobility. The purpose of these toys was not to promote the kind of play we talk about in this book; they were seen as preparing these children, through their imitation of adults, for their adult roles as leaders of armies.

With the Industrial Revolution and mass production, war toys became inexpensive enough to reach the hands of many more children who, until this time, primarily had homemade or improvised toys. First came miniature metal replicas of soldiers. Younger children probably used them to make up their own battles, but they could also be used in other ways. And older children could act out famous military battles; attention to strategy and to accuracy of detail probably took precedence over the actual fighting. Already, these war toys had moved children's war play a considerable distance away from the open-endedness of sticks and stones.

As the wars, enemies and uniforms of a country changed, so did the looks of the toy soldiers. But the basic nature of the toys did not change a great deal until 1859, when the mechanical cap gun was invented. Instead of just acting out miniature battle scenes, children were now channeled into taking on the fighting roles themselves, rather than acting them out vicariously through their toy soldiers.

This basic range of war toys remained more or less the same for decades. Then, in an expanding toy market that came with the widespread use of plastic in the 1950s, which made toys still less expensive, and the prosperity of the 1960s, manufacturers began to experiment with new kinds of war toys. In 1964, GI Joe, a doll-size soldier was introduced. For the first time, a doll was made attractive to boys by putting it in the uniform of a strong and masculine soldier. Children's war play was now directed toward identifying with the character of this soldier and making up fantasy battles for him. This toy was very popular until it became controversial in a climate of antiwar sentiment following the Vietnam War and was taken off the market in 1978.

It was also during this time that "mascot toys," dolls and soft toys that were replicas of popular characters on TV and in children's books, became big sellers. Disney characters, superheroes like Superman and then Batman, characters from the comic strip "Peanuts," and later, the Muppet puppets from "Sesame Street," were among the most popular. While often not associated directly with war toys, these mascot toys were largely successful because of the associations with popular childhood culture they called to mind in children. Children could now bring to their play with mascot toys what they had learned about the characters elsewhere. To add to their interest in acting out media characters, a few basic accessories for some of the mascots also gradually came on the market—for instance, a "Batmobile" for Batman—as well as some basic dress-up clothes which children could use to take on the roles of popular TV characters, like Superman's shirt and cape, and masks of Batman's and Robin's faces. These mascot toys and their paraphernalia served as a prototype for the linking of familar media characters with the marketing of toys.

In 1977, the link-up of media characters and toys led to a new concept in war toys. It was born out of the movie "Star Wars." A whole line of toys was marketed which included miniature fully equipped replicas of all the "good guy" and "bad guy" characters from the movie and all of their equipment. For the first time, instead of using whatever toys they had to invent their own scenarios from the bits and pieces of the movie that most caught their imagination, children were channeled into using purpose-specific toys to reenact the fantasy war they saw on the screen. They could do this especially well if they succeeded in collecting a lot of the toys in the Star Wars line. This major shift toward collecting toys and having all that was needed to replicate a story, provided the model for developing large lines of toys to accompany media events. It pointed the way for the transformation of war toys and war play that was soon to come in the eighties with the deregulation of children's television.

With deregulation, many war toy lines flooded the market. They were almost all directly tied to violent television cartoons and developed by toy manufacturers as a toy line/television program package. Now children could get daily instruction on what toys to buy and how to use them in their play. And the realism of the toys themselves helped to keep children confined within the focus of the plot. Among the television-linked toy lines to be introduced at this time was a completely redesigned GI Joe. Now called an action figure, the new GI Joe was more realistic, smaller, and less like a doll than its predecessor. Alongside it were over fifty other action figures and weapons, vehicles and accessories.

The concept of television-linked toys reached a new peak in 1987 with the introduction of toy weapons—for instance, Captain Power—that interacted electronically with the television. These weapons, activated by the TV set during battles, drew children into participating in the killing which in the past they had only been able to watch. They helped children actually learn and practice the fighting roles that they could continue to use in their play with the interactive toys after the show was over. And the recent rise to stardom of a new category of war toys—computer video games like Nintendo (the best selling toy of the 1988 holiday season)—now allows children to fight with the TV whenever they choose. Toys such as these should probably not even be called toys, because they leave no room for children to "play."

With interactive war toys, children could actually fight it out with the TV set.

The history of war toys reveals several general trends: from child-made to manufactured; from broad and generic to narrow and specific; from unrealistic to highly realistic; and, from open-ended (with many possible uses) to single-purpose. But in the last decade, there has been nothing short of a revolution in toys which has arguably brought greater change than in all the previous history of mass-produced war toys. It is a revolution which is marked by the channeling of children into imitating the violence that they have seen and the loss of children's power to control their own play.

Neo-war Toys

The bulk of the war toys around today are too close to the highly structured and realistic end of the toy continuum. Examples of such toys are endless. There are action figures that do one single grotesque thing—for instance, the Masters of the Universe character, "Mosquitor," has a button on his back. When pushed, the "blood" he has "sucked" from his victims churns around in his transparent stomach in a very realistic way. There are other action figures whose heads fall off or eyes pop out when hit in the "right" way. Today's toy designers seem to be stretching their imaginations to new heights in trying to come up with novel functions for toys—looking for the new twist that will get children to want it, that will get children hooked.

The distinction we made between play and imitation in the previous chapters is especially relevant when considering neo-war toys. In addition to limiting the dramatic play of young children by encouraging imitation rather than play (where they determine what they do and how they do it), today's single-purpose war toys encourage children to stay fixated on fighting, violence and even mutilation. And because these war toys are also connected to television characters and plots, play is further channeled into imitation of the violence seen on television, instead of into the rich dramatic war play children need to work out all the violence they are seeing.

Insofar as this new generation of war toys is influencing play, or more accurately, undermining play and turning it into imitation, we can argue that they should not be called toys at all; and that children should not play with them at all. But children want them, children won't give up trying to get them, and children will find a place to use them where they aren't banned, even if neo-war toys are banned from the home. Our interviews with children and parents reveal this time and time again. And as we discuss throughout this book, children have legitimate reasons—which grow out of societal forces as well as their own needs—to persist as they do. So, while we can and should try to influence the kinds and quantity of war toys our children have, both in the home and as a matter of public policy (which we will address in Chapter Eight), most of us will also have to find ways to affect how our children are using their war toys.

GUIDE
Supporting Play with Toys

Given what we now know about war toys, the challenge for us is to help children put war toys back in their proper roles as facilitators, rather than controllers, of play.

◆ **Know what kinds of toys your child is using.**

What are your child's favorite toys? Are they single-purpose ones or does he like toys he can use in many different ways? How many toys are tied to television shows? Are there a lot of war toys? Does he like other toys as well?

As you have seen, different kinds of toys foster different kinds of play and some kinds of play are more beneficial to children than others. Without even looking at how your child is using his toys, you can learn a lot just by taking a careful look at his toy shelf. If you find there is a preponderance of toys that are tied to TV shows, you may want to think about introducing an open-ended toy which could add diversity to your child's play. If you find mostly commercial toys, you may want to help your child begin to make some of his own toys.

One parent was surprised one day when he counted sixteen transforming toys in his children's collection. He decided to help his son and daughter make their own "transformers" out of cardboard and paper fasteners. Using cardboard and then wood, they eventually made a whole collection of creatures that transformed from robots to animals. (See illustration on the following page.)

◆ **Know how your child is using war toys and other play materials.**

Does your child spend a lot of his time at the early exploratory phase or does he get to more creative play? Does he play with one toy for a period of time, or flit from toy to toy? Does he use toys in the same way over time or in many different ways? Does he combine toys (and other objects) and use them together in a variety of ways?

Different children do have different styles and preferences when using toys. Some children prefer to spend much of their play time building with building toys. Others want to spend more time using their toys for pretend play. It will help to know your own child's general style of using toys, but whatever his preferences, you can look to see whether he uses toys in the same ways over and over or invents a variety of ways to use them. You can begin to learn how your child uses toys by taking periodic looks at his play as you go about your business and also by sitting back when you have a few moments and casually watching what is going on. See what patterns emerge over time.

Cardboard and brass paper fastener transforming toys can be a creative substitute for commercial "Transformers."

◆ **Hold the line on single-purpose war toys as long as possible; try to choose the most open-ended ones that will satisfy your child.**

Most families with young boys today do buy some of the contemporary war toys that are on the market. But the more you can limit these toys, the more developmentally useful your child's play is likely to be. When you are selecting a war toy, choose one that is as open-ended as possible—that is, one whose function and characteristics are not fully defined by its appearance or the toy box.

If you decide to buy a gun or other weapon, choose one of the less realistic ones that is not tied to a specific character or TV show, if you can. An old-fashioned cap gun or a water pistol leaves more room for creativity in play than a lasar gun that comes with specific instructions for its use.

◆ **Help your child use playthings in new ways.**

Children who have played mostly with single-purpose toys or who have a lot of toys tied in to television shows may need help thinking of new ideas for them. If your child uses a toy in the same way over and over or quickly becomes bored with it, he may need help learning to use his toys in different ways.

Offer ideas about new ways to use a toy. When your child is playing with "He-Man," a comment like, "My, you've used 'He-Man' so much he's really gotten dirty. Maybe you should give him a bath," can help your child add a new dimension to his play.

Try making suggestions which help your child get to know a toy or other play material better, to see more possibilities for what it can do. This works best when what you say grows out of what the child is doing. When your child is poking holes into play dough with his finger, comments like, "Look at all the holes you've made. Are there other kinds of marks you can make with your finger?" or "How many holes can you fit on?" helps her try something a little different.

◆ **Provide open-ended toys, props and materials to use with single-purpose war toys.**

One of the most effective ways of helping your child get away from imitating television scripts with his toys is to provide play materials which do not fit easily into the script. Both commercial toys and household objects can be useful. When you introduce something, try to have it connect in some way with what the child is already doing. You may even find that the new item distracts your child totally from his focus on fighting because it offers more interesting play possibilities.

You can offer Legos or playdough into a child's GI Joe play, for example. You can suggest how the new material might be used: "You can use your Lego to make a gun that's also a walkie talkie" or, "Maybe you can use these blocks for a stretcher when Joe gets hurt."

You can offer simple household objects into a play situation, such as pots and pans and empty plasic bottles and boxes. These "toys" are free, endlessly available, and help your child get away from the desire to buy more and more toys.

One parent described how after her son had been in a "battle" for a long time, she pulled out a giant pot and lid, along with a ball of yarn, and said, "Here, everyone must be very hungry after all that fighting." He took the pot and started "cooking" pasta for his army. Another parent took empty clear plastic bottles with squirt tops (from catsup and shampoo) and filled them with water and a few drops of food coloring. Her son delighted in going around outside and squirting his "poison" on everything (it was especially exciting when he could color the snow). And a third parent described how her two young children played for a whole afternoon with an old suitcase—dramatizing scenes with their action figures.

◆ **Help your child make his own toys and props for war play.**

Making his own playthings provides special challenges to your child. Deciding what to make, what to use to make it and then making it

Louis, who loved Star Wars action figures, ended up playing more with the Star Wars game he made with his father than with his store-bought figures.

look "right" and do the "right" things offers lots of opportunities for complex thinking, problem-solving, and feeling a sense of accomplishment. Making things also helps your child learn an alternative to asking for every new war toy he sees.

One mother, whose son wanted to get He-Man action figures, helped him to make them instead. They took chopsticks and paper, pens and tape and constructed a whole line of puppets. She helped him a lot on the first one, but after he had been through it once he took off on his own.

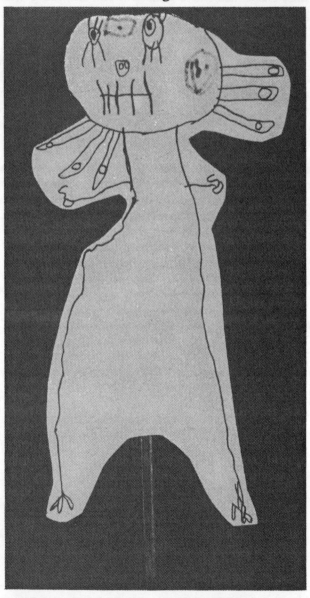

He-man puppet made from paper and chopsticks.

Often adults can help children to become involved in making toy "weapons" for play. Something as simple as a piece of cardboard can be all it takes. It's not very expensive to have a supply of paper, scissors, tape, markers, and pieces of cardboard and fabric readily available for children.

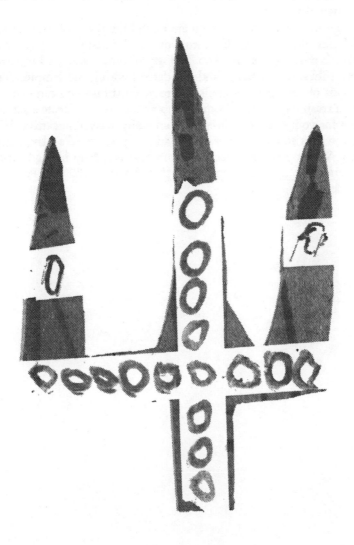

When children make their own weapons out of cardboard, their own ideas become a more important part of their play.

You can make costumes and masks together. Children love to dress up for play and costumes and masks help them with the process of developing meaningful roles. Paper plates, colored paper or old adult-size stocking hats can make wonderful masks. Old adult clothing, an old pillow case or pieces of fabric can be quickly transformed into costumes that suggest favorite roles or characters. (See Part II for specific suggestions.)

♦ **Look for scrounge materials and help your child invent interesting ways to use them.**

Scrounge materials (items which are bound for the trash but are clean and safe) can often be recycled into wonderful treasures for play: fabric remnants, boxes, pieces of foam and styrofoam, meat-packing trays, cardboard tubes, carpet scraps and out-dated flooring tile samples. There are all kinds of scrounge materials and recycled things you can save, find outside on trash day and get from neighborhood stores. Create a scrounge collection for your child and keep it in an easily accessible carton. When you see a way a scrounge item might add to your child's play, suggest it to him. When your child has a need in his play, help him go through the scrounge box and find something that fits the bill. (See Part II for specific ideas.)

5
Mama Won't You Buy Me a GI Joe?
Consumerism and War Play

The marketing of violence to children has become a big business. Violent television shows linked to war toys and licensed products all create in children an enormous desire to consume. Whatever interest children might have had for war play and guns in the past, it has been transformed in the 1980s by the revolution in toys and marketing techniques. Parents today often find that the questions they have about war play get lost in the daily struggles with their children over consuming.

The Birth of a Consumer

Children in the United States are born into a consumer-driven society and from an early age they are socialized into it. The family plays an important role. Starting at birth, relatives and friends often give children gifts on special occasions to express love. Children quickly learn to associate the acquisition of objects, especially toys, with a sense of being loved and with a general feeling of well-being. This sense of well-being often becomes associated with acquiring any new object.

The world outside the family also plays a very important role in socializing children to consume. In the course of daily life children are exposed to a multitude of marketing techniques specifically directed at them—from displays in stores, to the presence on food packages and clothing of logos associated with toys. But it is television that has become the most significant vehicle for promoting consumerism in the United States.

Media shapes ideas about what should be given or gotten and it sets the standards which children uncritically accept. Toy manufacturers spend millions advertising toys to children on TV in an effort to influence their early consumer habits. By the age of 18, the average child growing up in the United States today will have seen between 350,000 and 640,000 commercials on TV. Sometimes it only takes one viewing of a television advertisement for a child to become obsessed with desire for a toy which he recognizes at the store from 25 feet away. Children seem to decide, almost as if by instinct, that the toy in the ad is something they should ask for and want; that they may even need it in order to be happy and popular with other children. And even if they don't see an ad for a particular toy, their friends will see it and tell them about it or show it to them.

So very soon, along with the expectation of a continual stream of toys that signify love, comes the awareness, mainly from advertising, that "there are many toys out there that all have the potential to be owned." Martha, a parent of three children, saw what happened when she permitted television viewing one summer for the first time:

> They woke up at six o'clock in the morning and they would start in, all the children: "Can we go to the mall today? I want to buy . . . I need to get . . . " They started saying "mall" before they had their eyes open, before they had breakfast, before they were dressed!

Deprivation in the Midst of Plenty

Many people argue that, whether we are dealing with war toys or not, children are a special class of consumers and because of this, advertising and marketing techniques aimed directly at them are questionable from an ethical point of view. After investigating this issue in 1977, the Federal Trade Commission concluded that advertising to children is inherently unfair.

Yet in the eighties, the Federal Communications Commission removed every restriction that had been designed to protect children from commercial exploitation. They argued that the marketplace should determine the public interest: that parents and children should decide what shows they wanted to watch and what products they wanted to buy, and that these preferences should shape TV programming and toys. But in reality, the exact opposite occurs. Children's tastes and desires are shaped and fed by the media and toy world that surrounds them. They do not have the cognitive tools or past experience to use in making any choices other than those that they see.

It is not an exaggeration to say that the changes brought about by the FCC's rulings on children's television in the 1980s had profound effects—both immediate and long-lasting—on children. The lifting of restrictions led to the immediate collaboration between television producers and toy manufacturers. They created product-driven shows which were designed to sell products disguised as entertainment; these quickly became the norm in children's programming. With the lifting of the requirement to carry children's educational programming, the networks dropped their higher quality shows; all twenty people who had worked on children's programs in the CBS news department were gone after deregulation.

Sales of the TV-linked toys skyrocketed. The sale of toys grew from 7 to 14 billion dollars between 1980 and 1988. In 1984 alone, Mattell sold 35 million of the He-Man action figures (toys tied to the Masters of the Universe TV program); that meant 94,628 toy sales a day or 66.4 every minute. Toys that could not make it on TV dropped out of the market, and small toy companies that could not compete in the TV-dominated marketplace began to disappear. In a two-year period, Hasbro, the maker of GI Joe, took over Milton Bradley, Playskool and CBS Toys.

Most people who voiced concern about these trends (for instance, the lobbying group, Action for Children's Television) used the argument that young children could not distinguish between a TV show and an ad and that therefore, every toy-linked show was virtually an advertisement. While this is a legitimate and important argument, there are other issues which go much deeper.

For the first time in history, because of the TV-toy link-up, children were made to feel that they had to have certain toys in order to play. While in the past, children had grabbed whatever they could find for props to use in acting out stories they liked, now they were being told: "You should play GI Joe and to play it you need these action figures, these tanks, these props." This was a subtle but profound shift in the locus of control of play—away from children and into the hands of toy manufacturers. It built in a dependence on objects for play which was outside of children's sphere of control. It undermined children's basic sense of self-sufficiency in play.

In addition, manufacturers were producing whole lines of toys in order to increase profits. Every toy had one specific function so that a child would have to buy lots of them in order to play. The president of Hasbro stated that the GI Joe line, which has over fifty items, was designed to turn over completely every two years. This marketing strategy led children to begin to think in terms of quantities of toys. The emphasis in play shifted from "What can I do with this toy?" to "Can I get another one?" Toy supermarkets prospered, and for the first time in history, people shopped for toys by filling up shopping carts.

As we saw in the last chapter on toys, having large quantities of purpose-specific toys can have profound negative effects on the nature and value of play. In addition, toys with one function often leave children feeling unfulfilled. Once they've been used in the intended way and the novelty wears off, it's hard to figure out what to do with

Part of getting a new toy is finding a brochure for all the other toys in the line.

them next. Such toys can lead children down a path where they seek but cannot find the deep satisfactions of rich play. They can cause an insatiable desire in children to get more toys as a substitute for fulfilling the basic need to play. We would suggest that children end up experiencing feelings of deprivation, even as they sit among a vast array of toys.

But there is more to the story of how things changed for children under deregulation, because the new marketing practices did not stop with television and toys. Toy companies themselves, and other companies that bought licenses to use a toy line's logo, began to manufacture all kinds of other products using the logo from the TV character. GI Joe sneakers, Rambo party plates, CareBear underwear, Transformer pajamas and He-Man lunchboxes poured forth. In 1986, 51 companies were selling more then 120 products with the Transformer logo alone. Sometimes these products were not just for children; for example, Zip-Loc bags appeared with the Transformer logo on them and a decal inside. The obvious goal was to manipulate children into asking for the product because of its logo. Even though young children had no concern about the kind of plastic bags their parents bought, the logo said to the child, "Buy me, I am for you." And this practice worked. By 1986, the Toy Manufacturers of America estimated that close to 50 percent of the toy industry's sales were of licensed products. The toys, the television programs linked to them, and the products featuring the logos all became advertisements for each other.

From the child's point of view, the images from television and toys were literally everywhere. The typical child who went to school or daycare saw friends in He-Man T-shirts, carrying Transformer lunchboxes and wearing GI Joe sneakers. When he went into all kinds of stores with his parents, he spotted the licensed logos on many types of items. At home he watched about four hours of television a day where he would again see these images. And in his rather limited play time, he probably played with at least some of the TV-linked toys. If he had licensed pajamas, he could even continue his exposure to these images while he slept.

Parents Feel the Pinch

We hear many comments from parents about the problems they have over toy consumption. While they don't always know what brings this situation about, they often express discomfort about the numbers of toys that end up in their homes. They see their children have shelves full of toys but still seem bored and still ask for every new toy they see in an ad or at a friend's house. Here are a few examples of what parents say:

> Like many kids, mine have too much physical stuff. I didn't want to "spoil" them by giving them "too much" but somehow, "too much" has happened and now I'm trying to cut back. But it's hard—hard to undo what I've already done—they expect it, they seem to need it, and they always want more.

> Here's the vicious cycle we've gotten ourselves into . . . Julie begs for some new toy that she's seen, usually on television, or maybe a friend has it. She begs constantly; this is something she really *has* to have. She gets fixated on it, and hounds me for it. Finally I give in. We go buy it. Then she's happy for a little while, and so am I, except for the uncomfortable feeling I have that I am feeding a bad habit. But then before she's even played with it much, she starts in again with something else. She gets some other toy in mind and the whole thing starts up all over again.

> We were at the toy store to buy favors and other things for Raymond's fourth birthday party. When we got to the section with cups and napkins he noticed items with Ghostbusters on them, his favorite TV show of late. He got all excited about having a Ghostbuster party. He started looking for Ghostbuster everything—candles, plates, little action figures for prizes. I was caught by surprise. What he wanted

would have cost a fortune. I put my foot down and said it cost too much (but I really hated the idea). Then I said he could choose two Ghostbuster things for the party . . . he cried. He kept nagging me for more things right up to the party. It took some of the fun out of the whole thing.

In the eighties, manufacturers and TV producers have been very successful at bypassing parents when it comes to influencing the consumer habits of young children. It is now manufacturers who are calling the shots and the shots they are calling are destructive to children and their play. But if the marketing techniques are so harmful to children, then why have they succeeded so well? Why have children been so susceptible to the pressures to consume, so vulnerable to the marketing practices of the eighties? Looking at how the young consumer thinks can help us to answer these questions.

A Little Knowledge is a Dangerous Thing

Adults bring a lot of knowledge, experience and the ability to reason logically to their consumer buying decisions. When deciding whether to buy a new product, they can ask themselves questions about personal need: Is this something I can really enjoy or benefit from? Is it like other things I have? How is this new thing different or better? They can think about the economics of the purchase: How much does it cost? Can I afford it? Is it worth it? They can also ask themselves questions about the quality of the product: How does it compare with other similar products I've bought? What's it made of? How long will it last? And they can reflect on the marketing practices, including advertisements, that try to sell the product: Can it really do what the ad says it does? How is the manufacturer trying to get me to buy it? Is the ad giving me useful information or is it just trying to persuade me? What other information would help me with the decision?

Whether or not adult consumers choose to consider these questions, they have the capability to do so. But children do not. When they see a new toy or juvenile product—in an ad, at a store, on a TV program or at a friend's house—they have neither the context nor the cognitive sophistication to make the kinds of informed and logical judgments that adults make. And with today's marketing practices, this often gets children (and their parents) into big trouble.

Here's an example of how Aaron talks to his mother about personal need after having seen an ad for a Cabbage Patch doll:

Aaron: I want a Cabbage Patch doll. They're boys and girls, you know.
Mother: They're boys and girls?

Aaron: Yes. I want a boy.
Mother: You have "Adam." He's a boy doll. [The size of a Cabbage
Patch doll.]
Aaron: I want a girl.
Mother: You have "Baby Sarah." She's a girl. [A small baby doll.]
Aaron: But I want a large girl.
Mother: "Hannah" is a large girl. [A three-foot Raggedy Ann type
doll.]
Aaron: But I *need* a medium girl!

Once Aaron sees the ad for Cabbage Patch dolls, he wants one. Even
though he already has several dolls, he believes he needs it. His desire
for it prevails over his mother's attempts at rational argument. He is
able to carry on what seems like a logical discussion with her, but he
is unable to focus on the broader issue that concerns his mother—
whether he really "needs" a new doll. Aaron doesn't think about a lot
of information at once, but rather of one thing at a time. If the doll
is different in one concrete way from his other dolls, then it's a new
and different toy and offers new opportunities for play. He does not
look at the whole picture which includes the dolls he already has and
how this new doll might fit in.

This way of thinking can create real problems for young children
(and their parents) in a consumer society that offers an endless variety
of single-purpose toys. Children have no way of judging how many of
a particular kind of toy are a "reasonable" amount to have. There are
always toys children don't have that are a little different from what
they already have and children don't have the ability to sort out the
important from the unimportant differences among them. Aaron's
mother tries to help him see how the desired doll relates to those he
already has. She even draws on his new skills comparing big and little.
But Aaron is only able to think about how the new doll would be
different from what he already has, not the big picture.

Young children also have their own logic about economics which
prevents them from using knowledge of the money system to make
decisions about buying things. Here's Francis' idea about the
relationship between money and buying toys. Francis and his father
had this conversation just after he had unpacked his first "Star Wars"
action figure. He was studying the back of the package that showed
all the other characters.

Francis: I want to get *all* the "Star Wars" guys.
Father: We can't possibly get them all.
Francis: Why not?
Father: It would cost too much money. Where would we get all that
money?
Francis: I'll use my money.

Father: You don't have enough money. You probably have enough in your piggy bank to buy one more.
Francis: We could go to the bank to get the money.

Francis thinks what most young children think—that his family's money supply is fed by an unlimited number of trips to the bank. From first-hand experience, most children have observed how their parents walk into banks and come out with cash, so why not just go back to the bank if you need more money? The causal link between the bank and buying power is made at an early age but the complex and abstract concepts that underlie the family budget take a long time to develop.

Just as Aaron understood part of the whole picture about his doll collection, Francis understands only part of the picture about the money system. It is the most concrete part, the one he has seen. He uses this to explain why he could buy all of the toys he wants. Without understanding the whole situation about how money works, Francis does not understand why his father won't indulge his desires for an endless amount of toys.

Francis' desire for toys can flourish without the tempering effect of his cognition; he can experience the one-sided lust for things without knowing how reality limits acquisition. The more marketing practices stimulate his desire, the more tension Francis is going to experience (as well as his parents) as he encounters limits he is unable to comprehend. No wonder there is tension in Francis' family when a toy company like Hasbro, the maker of GI Joe, increases its advertising to children by over 100 percent in the first nine months after deregulation.

From Neils, we can get a glimpse at how hard it is for children to think about the quality of toys and how marketing practices influence their consumer behavior:

> One day at the store Neils spotted a particular small action figure he had just seen advertised on TV. He pleaded for it. It was cheap so I agreed to buy it, even though it looked flimsy. Well, about an hour after we got it home an arm broke off. Neils cried his eyes out. I comforted him for awhile and then said, "The people who made that ad were mean. They made the toy look great so you would buy it. They didn't care what happened once you got it home. They just wanted to get you to buy it. They're mean to children. Next time we see something you want in an ad, let's try to figure out if it's junky or not." Neils listened to my little lesson on advertising and he even said, "They shouldn't be so mean to children."
>
> About a week later, I was taken by surprise when Neils asked me if he could get another of the same kind of action figure. I tried to remind him about how upset he was when the last one broke. He

smiled and said, "That's okay. Now that it broke once I won't feel so bad the next time it happens!"

To start with, Neils doesn't think about the quality of the product he wants. He cannot know that the action figure that looks so powerful in a TV ad is made of cheap plastic and will break easily. Because of this, ads deceive Neils in a way that they do not deceive older consumers. When Neils' mother tries to help him learn about assessing the quality of toys from this experience, he shows that he has learned a different lesson: that toys are part of the throw-away world. Neils has learned that toys break easily, but they also can be easily replaced by making another purchase.

Neils' mother tries to enlighten him about the motives of manufacturers and he agrees that they are "being mean to children." But her ideas do not come naturally to him. He finds it very difficult to consider ulterior motives. They are internal processes he can't see. Things are how they seem on the outside. When he sees a toy that does amazing things through special effects in an ad, he believes that the toy can do this. He doesn't wonder if someone is trying to deceive him. He trusts in adults, and takes their word quite literally. Thus, the whole notion of advertising, which rests on the fundamental idea that someone is trying to sell you a product, escapes him. Because young children believe what they are told, they will accept an ad as the truth. Because of this, they are vulnerable to its message in a way that no adult is; and it is for these reasons that it is inherently unfair to advertise any products to children.

MaryAnn, whose son Rubin is obsessed with GI Joe, tells us how product licensing interferes with her efforts to teach him to be an informed consumer.

> I took Rubin to the store to buy a new pair of sneakers. There were lots of choices in the shoe store. We were looking them over, and I was trying to find a pair for Rubin that was going to last and would give his feet some support. Suddenly he started yelling with excitement. He was pointing to a pair of sneakers with a GI Joe logo on them. He was fervently begging to get them! They weren't at all the right sneakers for him, and I didn't want to buy them. I showed him all the ways the other ones were better . . . he couldn't think about anything but the GI Joes.

MaryAnn's experience illustrates another way in which children are susceptible to the marketing practices used today. The GI Joe logo carries a lot of power for Rubin. When he sees it on the sneakers it says to him, "These sneakers are for you!" Because of his egocentric thinking he has a hard time taking a point of view other than his own. And because of his tendency to focus on only one thing at a time, he can't think about any of the attributes of the sneakers mentioned by his mother, only the GI Joe logo.

All four of the children in the examples above were drawn into a world they could not fully understand. They were presented with advertisements and other marketing techniques which they did not have the tools to evaluate.

We can see that because of their special vulnerabilities which are a function of their stage of development, young children are easily exploited as consumers. While these vulnerabilities are not new, there is a new climate which permits manufacturers and advertisers to unleash techniques for capitalizing on them without restraint. To the extent that parents are trapped into buying products they would not otherwise buy, they are exploited by this marketing environment along with their children.

The Marketing of Violence to Children

It is not a small matter that specific images marketed to children literally fill their world; for, these images carry important messages and influence children in significant ways. It is an even more serious matter when the most common and powerful images marketed to children, especially to boys, are violent. While we have said that young children are interested in learning about violence, it is a very different matter to draw their attention to it by exploiting the vulnerabilities of their stage of development. This exploitation goes beyond the violent toys children use in their play, which is worrisome enough. It is present at every turn—when they are eating their lunch, going to sleep, brushing their teeth and putting on their underpants. Is it any wonder so many parents and teachers today say children seem preoccupied with violent images and want to get more and more violent toys?

The consumer patterns which today's children are developing from an early age lay the foundation for their relationship to material objects and their product preferences. Consumer products enter the developmental process so early that children believe that products play a central role in the quality of their lives. Even when market trends shift, for example when fewer TV shows linked to toys are produced in a particular season, the consumer habits that children have learned along with their propensity for violence fuels the sales of market items that can satisfy them. These deeper consumer habits which go beyond marketing fluctuations can explain the successful sales of many items not directly linked to television shows, such as Nintendo and Lazer Tag.

GUIDE
Consumer Education:
Empowering Children to Choose

If you haven't ended up with a crying child who wants to buy something in a store yourself, you have most likely witnessed such a scene. Parents are often caught off guard when this situation erupts; and children are taken by suprise too. They didn't know before they actually saw a treasured thing that they would desperately want to have it. Struggles like these are hard to respond to in the moment. In the midst of the commercial exploitation which exists in American society today and which is specifically aimed at children, we need to find ways to help children become informed consumers. The guidelines in this section will help you to think ahead about what is likely to happen over consumer issues with young children and what you can do to make things easier on your child and yourself.

◆ **Establish an open dialogue about consumer decisions.**
   It will be important for your child to feel that she can tell you about what she wants without getting a lecture or reprimand, even if it challenges your ideas and values. This does not mean that her desires will always need to be satisfied by a purchase; you will need to express your opinions, values and limitations too. And sometimes you may have to change your mind.
   After almost a year of living with a rule that only pistols and homemade guns were allowed at home, Bert (four years) had the following conversation with his mother:

> **Bert:** Mom, can I have a gun?
> **Roz:** You want a gun? What kind of gun?
> **Bert:** Yes, I want one that goes click when you pull the trigger.
> **Roz:** What do you want to do with it?
> **Bert:** Shoot and kill monsters . . . and bad guys too. They scare children.
> **Roz:** Is it to get people too?
> **Bert:** No. I won't hurt anyone. I mean . . . if someone runs into it, but only by accident. I learned how to use it at George's house, remember?
> **Roz:** Well it sounds like you've been thinking a lot about having a gun.
> **Bert:** Yes, I really, really want one. Please.
> **Roz:** You want me to think about getting you one again? You know we've talked about this before and I've told you how I don't like to

> see you pretending to fight all the time and some kids who come here
> have parents who don't like their children using guns.
> **Bert:** You keep it and ask parents if it's okay to get it out.
> **Roz:** And I've told you play guns that look too much like real guns
> can scare people because they don't know if they're pretend.
> **Bert:** There are clicking ones that don't look too real.
> **Roz:** You sure are willing to work out a way to have a gun with me.
> That's great! We'll both have a little of what we want? I think we
> should try it.

During this discussion, Roz and Bert are involved in a give and
take process. Roz provides concrete and very specific input about her
feelings and concerns that Bert seems to understand. She explains the
reasons for the rules she made in the past. But she also listens carefully
to what he has to say and he seems to trust that she takes his ideas
seriously. She is able to get Bert to agree to certain stipulations—about
the kind of gun he will get and how it will be used—that respond to
her values. They avoid getting into the kind of power struggle that
can often result when a child pushes a parent to buy something the
parent does not feel totally comfortable buying. There is no winner or
loser here. Roz and Bert are working together to find a solution that
is acceptable to both of them. The process they go through in reaching
the decision to buy a toy gun is at least as important as the decision itself.

♦ **When you want to stick to a limit about a certain toy, try to
find an alternative solution that meets similar needs.**
There will be times when you are not able to reach the kind of
agreeable resolution that Roz and Bert did. Children are often more
willing to accept the bans you stick to if they feel they have been heard
and that you have tried to take their point of view into account in
your decision. So it is still important to have the same kind of open
discussion Roz and Bert had.

Tom (five years old) has been asking for GI Joe toys for a long time.
In addition to not liking the toys, Ralph has supported the boycott
on GI Joe products that began in November of 1987 and has made
this clear to Tom. One day, Tom comes home from his babysitter's
with a mischievious look and a GI Joe sticker book that he got her to
buy him. Ralph and Tom have this discussion at dinner:

> **Ralph:** We need to talk about this sticker book. Remember what
> I've told you about GI Joe things. Look at them. They look so mean.
> All they do is fight all the time. Would you want any of them to be
> your friends?
> **Tom:** [Looking carefully at the characters] *No!*
> **Ralph:** But I'm upset most because of the boycott. I told you we
> promised other parents we won't spend any of our money on GI Joe

things so we can get the people who make them to change them. Even if I'm not there to tell you, you need to remember.

Tom: But we didn't spend *our* money. Jesse used hers.

Ralph: Yes, but the manufacturers still got the money to make more. We don't want them to get anyone's money.

Tom: [with a puzzled look] Oh, I didn't know. Will you throw the book out? I'll hate you if you do! You're so mean.

Ralph: I know you really want it and will be furious with me if you can't have it. What do you think I should do?

Tom: Please let me play with it *first*.

Ralph: It sounds like you think I should throw it out. Well, the people who made it already got the money whether we throw it out or not.

Tom: Maybe I could keep it but not get any more stickers with our money. I know! I could make my own stickers!

Ralph: How will you do that?

Tom: You know . . . with the white stickers I have that don't have anything on them.

Ralph uses this incident as an opportunity to educate Tom rather than punish him. He repeats his reasons for remaining firm in a way Tom can understand by using both the concrete characteristics of the GI Joes as well as the boycott (which is more abstract but which Ralph explains in very concrete terms). As he does this he seems to add to Tom's understanding of the boycott (Tom learns it means not spending *any* money, not just theirs). But Tom focuses most on what any young child would in this situation: what will happen to the book. Ralph allows Tom to express the concern and anger he feels about losing the book and acknowledges that his feelings are legitimate. Then he gets Tom involved in the process of working out a fair solution, without taking the one approach which would upset Tom the most (throwing out the book). In the end, Tom actually figures out an alternative solution that respects his father's wishes and values (he won't spend any more money on GI Joe), but which also meets his own desire to continue to use the sticker book (he'll make his own stickers). Through this active process the way is paved for Tom to take more responsibility for his own actions the next time he faces temptation.

◆ **Prepare for visits to stores in advance.**

It's unfair to ask children to go into a store, where they are literally bombarded with an overwhelming array of objects which all say "buy me," and expect them not to become completely caught up with the desire to consume. We know a parent who went to amazing lengths to avoid going into stores with her children in order to avoid the struggle. Another parent dealt with it by always letting his child make a purchase that cost less than one dollar. Both approaches helped to avoid the tensions and tantrums, but there are also less extreme measures you can take.

Your child will be in a much better position to cope with the shopping experience if you prepare her for what will happen at the store. Young children don't think about what it will be like in the store, how they will feel, or what they might see that they will really want until they are actually there. They don't imagine how you will react to their demands until they are actually demanding. But, you can help your child think things through on the way to the store. Tell her the purpose of the visit, what you plan to buy, how she can help you (for example, looking for a particular item you need), whether you intend to or are willing to buy something for her and if so, what. When possible, leave room for your child to have input into some aspect of the purchases that affect her (for instance, let her choose the color of her slippers or the size of the ball). And if she has any questions or objections about your plans, work them out before going in. When children know what to expect it's much easier for them to cope with the situation.

Once final plans are made, try to stick to them; stay away from impulse buying as much as possible. Impulse buying can teach your child that there is always the possibility that, if he argues or nags just right for something he sees, he might be able to get you to change the plan.

◆ **When you shop for a toy, use it as an opportunity for consumer education.**

Before any decision to buy a toy is reached, talk about it with your child. He will be in a much better position to use your input and his own knowledge and skills if it is discussed and worked out before he gets near the store. In the discussions, don't always expect your child to use the same logic that you do. We saw earlier what Aaron did with his mother's efforts to convince him he didn't need a Cabbage Patch doll. But good sense and logic will build gradually if you continue to work on the process together.

In discussions with younger children (and also with older children who have not had a lot of experience with this kind of discussion), focus on the most concrete aspects of a toy and how your child will use it: What will you do with it? Once you've done that what else can you do? Will it break easily? Will it do what the advertisement says it will? Can it hurt someone? Where will you be able to use it? When you give input, focus on similar concrete things: ways it might easily break; how it could hurt others; why it can only be used outside ("it's too noisy for inside"); how another toy can do more things; what from the ad the toy can and can't do ("it doesn't really make a big flash").

Gradually, as your child gets used to this kind of discussion, you will be able to work more abstract issues into the discussion. Is it like something else you have that you could use for the same purpose? Will it quickly become boring? Will it get you into trouble? Can you share it with other children? Have ads made you want to buy it? How well is it made? Are there other things the money could be spent on that would be more fun and interesting?

◆ **Help your child learn to evaluate her toys.**

When a toy disappoints your child in some way, use it as a basis for discussing the toy, the decision to buy it and what has been learned for the next time. While we saw how Neils' mother didn't make much progress when she tried to help him see that his cherished action figure broke because it was cheaply made, this kind of discussion does have an impact over time. Talk about such things as your child's experiences with a broken toy, a toy left abandoned on the toy shelf soon after it was bought, a toy that does not do what your child thought it would or a toy that frequently leads to trouble with friends or adults.

You can also help your child identify the "good" toys she has and what makes them good. Talk about favorite toys and what makes them so. Focus on the actual positive things she has done with them. Compare them with toys that haven't been so successful. Try a comment like: "You've had your Legos for a long time and you always come up with great new constructions. And they're always fun to use when your friends come over too." It will help children see why certain toys are worthwhile and convey your own values as well.

◆ **Establish predictable procedures and routines about toy buying.**

Much of the conflict that arises over acquiring toys is a result of a child not being able to understand what the boundaries are—what is and is not possible. When children know how toy buying decisions are made and how they can play a role in influencing those decisions, the situation often improves. There are specific ways you can establish the kinds of structures that help children know what to expect.

One parent kept a simple list of "the toys Jenna wants." Every time Jenna asked if she could have a particular toy, her mother said, "Let's put it on your toy list." They wrote it down together and made a little picture so Jenna could "read" her list. Periodically, they discussed the items on the list, what cost a lot of money and what didn't, what Jenna wanted most and why. Sometimes, they would decide to cross off some of the items on the list that were no longer very appealing. Then, when there was an opportunity to get a new toy, Jenna had a clear sense of her priorities as she used her list to make her choice. By keeping this list, Jenna quickly learned that while she couldn't have every new toy she wanted, she had a chance to talk a lot about what she wanted, and when she did get a toy, she had a reliable process for choosing it. All of this helped her feel much more in control of her own desires and consumer choices, while keeping the lid on the actual purchases.

Here is an example of a "toy requests list." You can use it to help control impulse buying.

Other parents have found it helps their children to know exactly when they will be able to get a new toy. We've already mentioned the parent who always let his child pick out a one-dollar toy on the weekly shopping trip. Another parent established a monthly trip to a toy store to buy a toy that cost not more than five dollars. We know of a child who only saw his distant grandparents twice a year and was allowed to choose a special toy with them during their visits. He knew that this was the one situation in which he had a big say in the decision and cherished this opportunity. Many other children find having routines for trading, borrowing and lending toys from cousins and friends is a way to have access to desired toys without feeling every desired object has to be purchased. It can also help egocentric children think about giving and the needs and desires of others, rather than focusing only on what they want and getting more things for themselves.

It probably won't matter very much which specific mechanisms you use to create structure for your child. What will make a difference is that when she wants something she knows what to expect and what she can do; then she won't have to work it out with you each time.

There is one technique we recommend trying to avoid: offering to buy a toy for your child as a reward for good behavior. Using toys as a reward only feeds into the belief in children, already fostered too much by society, that they need new toys and other objects in order to feel good about themselves and what they do. It also contributes to a kind of power relationship with you that can interfere, in the long run, with your child's ability to develop internal controls about consumer decisions.

◆ Help your child learn about the role of money in the toy buying process.

As we discussed earlier in this chapter, a major source of tension between children and parents is the difficulty children have understanding money—where it comes from and how much it takes to buy something. While trying to help your child make consumer decisions by emphasizing the role of money will rarely make much sense to her, you can begin to help her build an understanding of money slowly.

At first, children think about the price of a toy not in terms of specific numbers, but rather in relation to it costing a lot or a little money or too much money. Some children relate the price of a toy directly to its size—big toys cost a big amount of money and small toys cost a small amount. They may also think that a toy paid for with four quarters is more expensive that one paid for with a one-dollar bill—because four is more than one. At this stage, there isn't a lot you can do to teach the specifics of money. But you can do little things to try to expand their thinking, like pointing out that a particular small toy costs a lot and a big toy costs a little or the relative price of different toys (for instance, three of those cost the same amount as one of these).

As children begin to understand more about numbers and quantity, there is more you can do—but it will still have to be tied to concrete experience. You can help children learn about how much a particular amount of money can buy. For instance, if your child gets some money of his own (a gift, for example), talk about the things his amount of money can and can't buy.

By the time children are about five or six years old, a regular allowance of some sort can help them learn about the relationship between money and toys as well as how to budget their money. At first, most children spend their allowance the minute it arrives, but over time they can learn to plan and save up for bigger purchases.

When children start having access to their own money, it may be a time to let them have a bigger say about what is purchased than when you are using your own money. This is often a tricky business. Many parents have found themselves caught in the dilemma of telling a child that he can do what he wants with his own money, only to see him buying something they have always forbidden. (One parent who had always forbidden GI Joe told us how her twelve-year-old son got a paper route and soon had over fifty action figures in his GI Joe toy collection!) There is no easy solution here, but sooner or later, children will decide how their own money is spent. So, it's probably better to help them gradually learn to assume that responsibility rather than have it happen all at once.

◆ **Help your child become an active and informed consumer of advertisements.**

We have already mentioned ways to help children learn about ads by making comparisons between what toys actually look like and do versus how they appear in ads. There are also other things you can do.

Try watching and talking about TV toy ads with your child. With younger children, talk about very concrete things: how big the toy really is; how fast it goes; whether it really can light up and make the special noises. With older children discuss the ad's special effects so he knows what's real in an ad and what isn't. Help him try to figure out how the special effects are created. Talk about why the children in an ad, be it for a toy or some other product like cereal, seem so happy and excited; does your child think he would feel so happy in the same situation?

Children often know when they have been cheated by a toy or the advertisements for that toy. In most cases they learn just to accept the injustice. Yet the feelings of disappointment can linger. We know of a teacher who asked her third-graders to write about a time a toy had not lived up to their expectations. She was amazed to find that every child in the class, without hesitation, wrote a detailed and emotional account of this experience.

Tell me About a toy or food that you saw advertised on t.v or in a magazine. That, when you bought it wasn't as good.

I got the G.I. Joe Aircraft carrier and it stinks. In the commercial it held 18 jets and the super structure has 21 rooms. In real life it holds 2 jets and the Super Structure has 9 rooms.

Liers!!!!!!

why did they have to lie so much? why couldent they lie only a litel bit? why couldent they make it a litl more realistic instead of a stupid piece of junk with holes in the bottom?!!!!!

Here one child talked about how he was disappointed by an advertisement.

By the time your child is about five years old, you can begin to help her learn there are definite actions she can take when she has a legitimate complaint about a toy or other product. Return the item to the store together and explain to the salesperson exactly why you are bringing it back. Or, write a letter together to the manufacturer saying how a toy has not lived up to its claims and why your child thinks that is unjust. In most cases you'll find that your child gets an immediate response from the public relations department of the toy company, an experience which is very satisfying for most children. You can also write letters of complaint about products to consumer protection agencies and organizations and toy stores. Taking some kind of specific and positive action when a toy does not do what has been promised helps children learn to be consumer activists—to feel empowered to make a difference in their consumer world.

6
"Whatever Happened to Annie Oakley?"
Girls, Sexism and War Play

Many adult women in the United States today engaged in war play as children and remember it with obvious feelings of enjoyment and pleasure. They tell stories of their playground games, usually with boys, of soldiers, cowboys or cops—games of running, hiding, shooting and catching each other. And they tell us about the sense of adventure and meaningful social connection they experienced.

In our many discussions with parents about their children's play today, they are almost unanimous in their observation that war play is now an activity almost exclusive to boys. They look at their children's play and ask why children often have such a clear but narrow idea of what is expected for their sex and why they adhere to it so rigidly. They say their sons play GI Joe, He-Man, Ghostbusters, or Teenage Mutant Ninja Turtles while their daughters play My Little Pony, Barbie, dress-up, and house. Girls imitate sterotypic female behavior—concern about their looks, helplessness, passivity; and, as one parent said, "being saccharine sweet, goodie-goodies"; boys put aside nurturing behavior as they fight and defeat the bad guys. Parents also tell us that they get into the same kinds of arguments with their daughters about buying Barbie dolls and make-up that they have with their sons over action figures and toy weapons. And, they say that it is getting harder for their boys and girls to find common ground for playing together.

Many veteran teachers of young children report that the division in play between the sexes is occuring at earlier ages than it did a few years ago when there were more girls in the block area and more boys playing "house." They see less interaction, in general, between girls and boys. And today, both boys and girls seem to carry stronger masculine and feminine images with them as they go about the classroom—made more salient by boys in camoflage clothing and girls in "frills." Teachers tell stories of boys turning everything at their disposal into guns and making shooting noises as they paint at the easel to an extent they didn't do in the past, while girls increasingly use the same paint to polish their fingernails and hobble around the classroom all day wearing high heels from the housekeeping area.

These parents and teachers correctly point to a climate of sexism in the eighties that envelops their children, especially through the media and toy culture. The trends of the sixties and seventies toward helping children expand their gender roles beyond narrow stereotypes in play, toys, and child-rearing practices, in general, have been replaced by a toy and play culture which is more gender-specific than ever and which has both boys and girls spending more of their time in gender-specific play than ever before.

The Great Divide

In the climate of deregulation which allowed for the linking of children's television programs to toys, girls were as ripe an audience for advertisers as were boys. Using many of the same marketing strategies developed for boys, TV producers and toy manufacturers created a parallel market for girls. What has emerged is a set of television programs and toys linked to them which are as stereotypically "female" as the fare being offered to boys is stereotypically "male." Reading the promotional material from the backs of the packages of a My Little Pony and a GI Joe toy, reveals just how much the division between the sexes is exaggerated, almost to the point of caricature, by the toy industry.

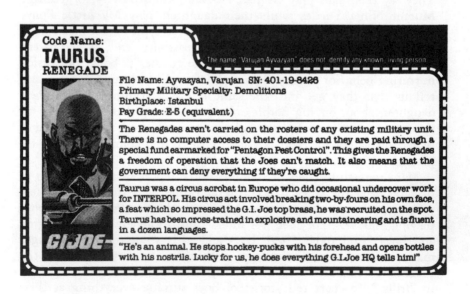

Code Name:
TAURUS
RENEGADE

The name "Varujan Ayvazyan" does not identify any known, living person

File Name: Ayvazyan, Varujan   SN: 401-19-8426
Primary Military Specialty: Demolitions
Birthplace: Istanbul
Pay Grade: E-5 (equivalent)

The Renegades aren't carried on the rosters of any existing military unit. There is no computer access to their dossiers and they are paid through a special fund earmarked for "Pentagon Pest Control". This gives the Renegades a freedom of operation that the Joes can't match. It also means that the government can deny everything if they're caught.

Taurus was a circus acrobat in Europe who did occasional undercover work for INTERPOL. His circus act involved breaking two-by-fours on his own face, a feat which so impressed the G.I. Joe top brass, he was recruited on the spot. Taurus has been cross-trained in explosive and mountaineering and is fluent in a dozen languages.

"He's an animal. He stops hockey-pucks with his forehead and opens bottles with his nostrils. Lucky for us, he does everything G.I.Joe HQ tells him!"

GIJOE

s Tiffany™
medallion, hairpick,
...lie
...and

Ages:
Small part...
hazardous...
under 3 y...

My Little Pony
Princess Ponies™

Princess
Tiffany™

Princess Primrose™

Princess Primrose™

The night of the Pony Ball arrived!
Princess Tiffany smoothed her gown
as she prepared to make her royal entrance.
But as she reached the staircase, her heel
caught the hem of her dress, and she
stumbled down the stairs! Everyone rushed to
help, but all Tiffany could do was cry. Suddenly, Princess
Starburst had an idea! She waved her magic wand, and
Tiffany's teardrops turned into sparkling diamonds that
covered her gown. Princess Sparkle waved her wand, a
lovely bouquet of flowers appeared in Tiffany's hand.
Tiffany smiled, ready to try her entrance again.
Everyone agreed it
was a splendid
evening after all,
especially
for Tiffany.

Princess
Primrose™

3

The programs and toys developed for girls today have two central themes—feelings and appearance. The feeling theme focuses on "gentle" feelings such as caring, sharing and nurturance, or sadness and helplessness. In a typical line of toys, each feeling is expressed through one specific toy. One example of a "feeling toy" line is the "Care Bears," a collection of fluffy stuffed animals for children from infancy on up. Each Care Bear resembles the others, but has been assigned one specific personality trait by the manufacturer and always behaves according to that trait. There is "Cheer Bear," "Tenderheart Bear," "Share Bear," "Funshine Bear," "Friend Bear," etc. The Care Bears live in "Care-A-Lot" and have a line of relatives, who live in the "Forest of Feelings."

As with boys, when girls play with their single-purpose "feeling" toy, especially after having watched the TV show that goes with it, their play is channeled into imitating the feeling suggested by the toy. It can be hard to do anything else. The repertoire of feelings and behaviors that a girl might express in her play is narrowed. The Care Bears define almost exclusively light and happy feelings to act out; "My Little Ponies" are sometimes allowed to also feel sad and helpless, like "Princess Tiffany" did. Stronger emotions such as hostility and anger, along with the stronger actions that might accompany them, are reserved for boys' toys and television programs. Interestingly, all of the current lines of toys for girls appear in mute pastel colors— primarily lavender and pink. The bold reds and blacks are reserved for the boys. The message to both girls and boys about what feelings and actions they should express comes through clearly.

The other major theme found in the television programs and toys aimed at girls is appearance. Toys lines such as "Barbie" and "Jem" are typical examples. The focus of all of these dolls is on clothes, hairstyles and make-up which reflect the latest fashions of the glamorous and affluent. Mattel, the manufacturer of the Barbie toy line, claims to be the world's largest producer of "women's wear" today. One standard for beauty is imparted to girls through such toys, and no real diversity in terms of ethnicity or body type. There are many dolls in each line and each doll looks slightly different and has a slightly different personality. Each series has a lead doll who is sexy and thin, and usually blond. One or two dolls have darker skin and hair but otherwise all the dolls closely resemble the lead doll.

These toy lines, recommended for girls as young as two or three years, are replacing "baby dolls," which have almost disappeared from the shelves of many toys stores. Instead of playing "house" with dolls and acting out family roles from their own experience, girls are now spending play time dressing up their Barbies and pretending to be glamorous teenagers and adult women. One grandmother told us that in response to the question, "What do you want to be when you grow up?" her four-year-old grandaughter who loved Barbies replied, "A teenager!"

Often feeling and appearance themes are merged into one toy line. "My Little Pony" is a good example with at least thirty different ponies to collect. In addition to "Princess Tiffany," there is "Trickles," who will "steal your heart away," and "Confetti," who is "stylish and cheery in any parade." As with the example from "Princess Tiffany" quoted above, each pony comes with superficial little stories on the package which reflect its predetermined personality. Each pony has a long mane and tail of a different color from the others, and comes with a special comb. And then, to help girls perfect their pony-grooming techniques, there is the popular "Brush Me Beautiful Beautique" which is part of the line, and a "Pretty Parlor" where "all the Rainbow Ponies love to get dolled up in front of the mirror." Many parents report how their daughters just sit for long periods of time, either combing their ponies' manes or cheerfully bouncing them around a room. Then they ask to collect more.

A more recent trend is the rapid expansion in the sale of make up for girls—play lipstick, eye make-up, false fingernails. The popularity of make-up may be an outgrowth of girls' interest in appearance and grooming created as they played with toys like My Little Pony and Barbie. Sometimes the make-up is made to seem like a "toy," perhaps to make it seem more appropriate (to parents) and interesting (to little girls) than if it were just make-up. A classic example is a line of toys called "Adorable Transformables" recommended on the package for girls ages four and over. One item is a necklace with a little toy dog that turns into a lipstick. This toy line taps into a young child's natural interest in how things can change from one thing to another and be more than one thing at the same time (already capitalized on by Hasbro with the Transformers which are popular with boys) and is also used to market all kinds of make-up to girls.

The underlying messages conveyed to children by the toys of today divide the sexes. In so doing, they keep children from bringing their most significant experiences and their most complex feelings into their dramatic play. Boys' toys channel them into being strong, dominant and competitive. They involve boys in life and death issues and keep them active and busy trying to "save the world." Girls' toys channel them into being passive, helpful and "pretty." They foster play that trivializes emotions and leaves very little of substance for girls to make use of in their dramatic play. They lock play into a pastel world of sugar-coated plots and compartmentalized, partial feelings.

Girls seem to love the toys that are marketed for them as much as boys love theirs. After Nintendo, Barbie was the best selling toy line during the 1988 holiday season. It's not by chance that the marketing of sexism to children has been so successful—there are developmental reasons that help explain it.

Which Came First—the Chicken or the Egg?

Many parents who try to raise their children to be as free of sex-role stereotypes as possible still find their children showing early preferences for sex-typed toys and play. By the time most children are two years old, parents begin to notice differences—boys seem to be drawn to guns and fighting and girls are attracted to dolls and housekeeping play. One father put it this way:

> I'll tell you how it all began. When Derrick was two years old, he started at the community daycare center, a small cooperative daycare. There was lots of talk among the parents about what kind of play we wanted to encourage in our kids. We had made a decision that we did not want aggressive play, and certainly no war play in the daycare. We talked a lot about it in evening meetings. I remember being uncomfortable that the discussion always involved boys. One father got very upset when his son bit a graham cracker and pointed it at his father and said, "Bang!" The father wanted to know who had taught this to his son. That was my first awareness that maybe it would happen whether we wanted it or not. And almost immediately thereafter, I became aware that Derrick was using a lot of aggression in his imaginative play. Then he started picking up broomsticks and other objects and shooting and asking for a gun. And I said "no guns." And he was picking up all kinds of objects and shooting. Then he started asking for every toy gun he saw.

Parents often take observations of their children like this one as a sign that the differences between girls' and boys' interest in war play must be due to differences in the genetic make-up of males and females, not what happens in the environment. Other parents are convinced that their children quickly learn what boys and girls should do from television, toy packages, their preschools and friends. One mother who had felt relatively successful at avoiding stereotypes with her three-year-old son, told a poignant story about sending him happily off to daycare with his prized "Care Bears" lunchbox. He was jeered and laughed at by the other boys for having a "girls' lunchbox." Parents like this one are especially critical of what the current environment is doing to their children and think the differences they observe have little or nothing to do with the inherent nature of boys and girls.

In either case, there seems to be little doubt that both girls and boys are especially drawn to the sex-specific toys that are intended for their gender, and neither is very interested in the other's choice, at least not for long. And parents often struggle over why this is so.

A major task of the preschool years is to develop a definite and positive gender identity. At a very early age, about eighteen months, boys and girls learn a label for their own sex. Immediately they try to figure out what their label means. They begin to define two separate categories, one for the behaviors of the sex they are and one for the sex they aren't—"If I'm a girl and not a boy, what do girls do that's different from what boys do?" Children look to the world around them—their families, other children, schools, books and the media—for information that will tell them how to define their girl and boy categories.

Young children base what they think on how things look and they do this as they try to work out their categories for gender. Because men's voices are deeper and their bodies are bigger, young children often think that men are more powerful and less nurturing. So just as young children think that a tall woman of twenty-five is older than a short woman of fifty, they also will tend to think that the bigger person is more powerful, important and mightier.

It is often puzzling to adults that even when children are raised in environments as free from gender stereotypes as possible, they still seem to form fairly stereotyped images of gender roles in the early years. But given what we have just said about how young children think and their early need to define gender, this phenomenon is not necessarily surprising. Even when boys see males in nurturing roles, they will continue to dichotomize gender roles to some extent and will still associate nurturance primarily with females. And they will still often look for male roles and behaviors to use in defining their gender that provide an alternative to nurturing. A similar phenomenon also occurs with girls. It is only as children get older and their thinking becomes less rigid and more complex, that their early experiences with a wide range of male and female roles are likely to get more fully integrated into their ideas about gender.

One mother, a smoker, described an episode at the airport with her three-year-old son, Jackson. A man walked up and put a cigarette out in a nearby ashtray. Jackson laughed and said, "That's funny." When the mother asked what was funny, he replied, "Men don't smoke cigarettes, they smoke pipes!" She thought back to Jackson's experiences with smokers and realized the cigarette smokers he knew were all women.

Jackson's reaction shows how quickly and automatically young children pick up information from their environment about gender roles that even most adults don't notice. Whether the sex differences in a child's environment are subtle or highly pronounced, it seems that children will find ways to define male and female categories for themselves.

Both boys and girls, by the very fact that they are born a boy or girl, search for gender models to identify with—to tell them what they should be like. Girls try to find ways to be like their mothers, and have much immediate experience to draw upon because mothers (and other females) are still the primary caretakers of most children. They establish their gender identity by trying to be like the people with whom they have had the most experience and imitate the behaviors they have experienced most from that person—for instance, nurturance and affection.

Boys, on the other hand, have a more complex task. They must form a gender identity that is different from that of their usually female caretaker. They must separate from their mothers (or other females), and from the nurturing behavior they received as babies. They go looking for what it is that males should do and they usually focus on behaviors that are as different from the nurturance they associate with females as they can find. In addition, boys may feel a level of stress, frustration and even anger as they try to move away from their mothers that girls do not experience. Behaviors which help them feel strong and able to take care of themselves without their mothers and which help them express their anger and frustration are likely to be especially appealing to boys.

Toys and pretend characters can respond to young children's genuine need to work on their gender identity. So children will often be attracted to those playthings which help them work out their male and female roles. Dolls, cuddly stuffed animals and tea sets are appealing to girls because they can help them identify further with the female behaviors with which they are most familiar, such as nurturance. Toy weapons and superheroes offer boys the very clear alternatives to female models that they are seeking, as well as the opportunity to express some of the angry feelings they might have about having to become different from their mothers.

Today's toys are likely to be especially appealing, and even seductive, to children. Not only do the characters and toys serve the function of helping children work on their gender identities in play; they can make this job even easier by demonstrating with TV shows exactly how to be a "boy" or "girl" with the toy. What's more, the information appeals to children because it is presented in terms that match young children's thinking very well—for instance, in terms of opposites, exclusive categories and concrete attributes. The gender distinctions provided by media images and toys make it easy to divide the world up into neat compartments where the differences between males and females are graphic and simple, where good guys are always good and bad guys bad, where males are always strong and powerful and females always weak and in need of rescue. In addition, in keeping with children's need for concrete information, the exaggerated muscles and superpowers of male TV and toy figures show clearly what men do; the exaggerated sexuality and helplessness of female characters show what women do. And, of course, because there are such clear sex distinctions in the behavior of male and female characters (which is just what children are looking for), neither sex does what the other does.

To say that gender divisions in playthings can help children meet their need to work out their gender roles in no way lets the manufacturers of today's sexist toys off the hook. For it is one thing to help children work out their gender roles through play and another to exploit for profit the questions they are having about their identity.

The Cost of Pink and Blue

In every culture parents want their children to develop a healthy gender identity—to feel good about the gender they are and what their gender does. Rigid divisions in the behavior of boys and girls aren't necessary for this to occur. Different cultures define what's appropriate behavior for males and females in very different ways. Cultures also differ in how narrowly or broadly they define behavior for each sex and in how much overlap in behavior they allow between the sexes—that is, whether there are many ways or a few ways males and females are taught to be alike and different from one another. Despite this diversity among cultures, children everywhere usually develop positive views about their gender. One of the key ways they do this is through play.

One way children use their play is to develop ideas about how they should behave as girls and boys and to try out adult gender roles. Then, they bring what they've learned to the "real" world. Those studying sex-role stereotyping in play fifteen years ago in the United States pointed out how differences in the play and toys of boys and girls were having negative consequences for both sexes. Even then it was argued that all children were learning a skewed set of ideas and behaviors as a result of their gender.

Researchers recognized then that traditional girls' and boys' play led to learning very different lessons. Girls worked on social skills such as cooperation, empathy and obedience in their traditional domestic play. These are skills which are useful to everyone. They help a child form positive relationships with others and get along in groups and in school. And from their traditional rough-and-tumble and war play, boys learned to argue and fight, to stand up for themselves and to be strong. But what was dawning on educators and parents was what each gender was *not* learning from their traditional forms of play. Girls were not learning how to be independent, resourceful or assertive; how to take risks and express controversial views. And boys were missing out on a whole range of play experiences which would help them to express their tender feelings, experience both giving and receiving of nurturance and learn to cooperate and get along with others. Both sexes, it was recognized, suffered, as their play reduced the range of experiences possible for each to have.

In addition to the social attitudes and skills learned, boys and girls are also learning different physical and cognitive skills from their different forms of play. When girls quietly play house with dolls and put on make-up they may be developing small muscle control and eye-hand coordination, but they are not developing the large motor skills that boys are as they run around shooting and capturing each other. Girls learn how to make their bodies look attractive, while boys are making their bodies physically fit. As a result, in school, girls may be better prepared than boys to sit still and do small-motor activities such as writing; but boys are learning some skills from their play which give them other advantages over girls at school.

When a boy builds a weapon with a toy like Legos, he is learning about: spatial relationships ("How does this part relate to the whole construction?" and "Where do I put it to make it do what I want it to?"); cause and effect ("If I add this piece, what happens?"); quantity ("How many of these do I need to make it the same size as that?"); and, strategy ("How can I move the pieces around to make this be the gun I want?"). Through this, boys are developing a knowledge base about the physical world—how it works and how to control it—which can help them in such school subjects as math and science. As girls dress and feed dolls and put on make-up, they have far fewer opportunities to develop this kind of knowledge. These differences can have specific consequences for the academic strengths and weaknesses boys and girls develop. This may help explain why the term "math phobia" has been used to describe many girls' negative reactions to doing math. Certainly differences in school performance between girls and boys can have a considerable impact on later adult interests, abilities and career choices.

These earlier concerns about how sex-role stereotyping prevents children from reaching their full potential are still valid today. But as already discussed, now there are new ingredients which heighten the stereotyping in children's play and make the cost to children even greater.

Too Much Sugar and Spice Isn't So Nice

When play is rich, children have a chance to construct flexible and broad gender identities and to develop a wide range of human potentials.

Even though girls and boys did see plenty of gender stereotyping and had gender-specific toys fifteen years ago, their play could be flexible—they could find some room to experiment and some common ground for playing together. Girls played cowboy and soldier, and boys tried on aprons and played house—at least some of the time.

But today this kind of play is in jeopardy. The toy and television industries are using their combined strength to divide the play of boys and girls in a way that is different from the past. Television cartoons contain more gender-stereotyped content than they ever have. Advertisements are explicitly designed for either girls *or* boys; one TV ad for army paraphernalia starts out with an announcer's voice calling, "Boys—Look!" Toys linked to television programs trap children into imitating stereotyped behavior. The single focus of many single-purpose

Today, it is the very rare girl who likes to play soldier or cowboy.

toys is often a highly sex-stereotyped one, such as combing hair or flexing muscles. This combination of factors makes it much harder for all children to move beyond gender stereotypes—to branch off from them in ways which enable their own ideas about gender to develop. These narrower gender categories affect children's self-images, the activities they decide to try, and therefore, what they learn and their perceptions of their own abilities and potentials.

GUIDE
Getting Beyond Stereotypes:
Helping the Whole Child Grow

Because so much of play with the single-purpose toys of today is gender stereotyped, many of our suggestions in the previous chapters for helping to expand play will positively affect children's sex-role stereotyped play behavior. Here we focus on the more direct ways you can try to combat the gender stereotypes children learn through play, so that they may use their play to develop the full range of human potentials.

◆ **Help boys and girls to play together.**

Girls and boys can be helped to get beyond narrow gender stereotypes when they share their ideas, interests and skills together in play. Yet, when girls' and boys' play is so different, the opportunity for play to spontaneously arise between them is small. Even when the opportunity does arise, boys and girls may have a hard time finding common ground for play. So you may have to get actively involved helping them find materials and activities they can comfortably share.

One parent described watching her daughter sitting on the front steps of their apartment building next to a male friend about the same age. Holly had her Barbie dolls, and Michael had his GI Joe figures and tanks. Each held their own dolls as they eyed those of the other. They looked as if they wanted to play together, but just ended up sitting there. In a situation like this an adult could help Holly and Michael get started by offering some neutral play material which is not identified with either sex, such as a small set of farm animals, some Legos, or playdough. Or, perhaps she could suggest a different activity, such as a cooking or art project.

◆ **Help both girls and boys to expand their play behaviors and skills beyond stereotypes.**

Both boys and girls today are missing out on important play experiences which contribute to their development as whole people. Girls need active, robust play where they feel emotionally strong and powerful and can develop large muscles. They need the chance to mastermind and create structures with building materials. Boys need to express feelings of vulnerability and caring in play, and to try out roles involving nurturance.

If a girl is hooked on commercial toys, look for ways to bring in more creative toys she can use along with them. Encourage her to build things she can use with her commercial toys. If she likes Barbie, give her a carton, wallpaper or tissue paper, scissors and glue to build Barbie a house. Help her use wood scraps, clay or Legos to make simple furniture. If she likes My Little Pony, suggest she build a corral for the horses out of Popsicle sticks and chick peas or playdough.

Girls need access to building materials, such as Legos, Tinkertoys, and blocks. Some girls might enjoy building projects that are collaborative as opposed to working alone, and it's important to consider this possibility when encouraging girls to build.

There are other activities that can enable girls to enjoy using their large muscles while they also contribute to an expanded self-image. One possibility is simple woodworking tools like a hammer. Even a very young girl can learn to hammer large nails. An old tree stump is perfect for this purpose, but large wood scraps work well too. A large paintbrush and a bucket of water make a wonderful set-up for "painting the house." All large motor activities, from activities at the park to building "obstacle courses" with furniture at home, contribute to girls' physical and psychological growth.

We have already discussed ways to encourage boys, who favor TV-based war toys, to expand their play and explore a wider variety of playthings. As you're working on this try to include suggestions that involve nurturance and prosocial behavior. For instance, supply them with props for dramatic play that encourage nurturance and expression of feelings, such as pots and pans, bandages, baby blankets and dolls other than action figures. Help them to develop nurturing behaviors with their action figures, such as dressing them up, feeding and bathing them and putting them to sleep.

◆ **Help children develop an awareness of sex-role stereotypes.**

Sexism is a very abstract concept that children will come to understand over many years' time. But even at an early age, adults can help them begin to think about this idea in their own ways and as it connects to their immediate experience.

Here is an example of how Rena helped Marcel and Jocelyne (aged five and six years) think about sexism as they were watching "Ghostbusters" on TV. There were four male characters and one female character on the show. The men went out and fought the ghosts while the woman remained at the office.

> Rena: How come all the Ghostbusters are the men? Why aren't there any women?
> Marcel: Because someone needs to stay at headquarters to take care of things and answer the phone.
> Rena: And why is it always the woman?
> Jocelyne (thinking seriously): She doesn't have a Ghostbusting Machine (a backpack for busting ghosts that all the men have).
> Rena goes into the kitchen and starts preparing the meal. Jocelyne comes running in yelling: "She did go get the Ghosts! Someone else was knocked out and she took his machine and she went out and busted ghosts!"

Rena's questions about the role of women on this cartoon were important enough to Jocelyne that they stayed with her as she watched the show. Rena put the question in terms that the children could understand, that men and women are doing different things, rather than a more abstract remark such as, "What a sexist program!"

Talking with children about their direct experience with stereotypes as Rena did is most meaningful to them. If a child likes Rambo, you could ask "Is Rambo like the men you know? What other things do the men you know do?" This kind of question will help children to relate their own experience with fathers and other men to the media and toy images of maleness they see.

Some of the most glaring sex stereotyping children see is on advertisements aimed at them. In most toy ads it is obvious whom the toy is intended for. In addition, boys and girls are often depicted in extremes: boys are shown fighting and shooting, while girls are shown combing hair or grooming themselves. These blatantly sexist images make good subject matter for discussion with children because they are clearly defined and easy to grasp. Questions and comments should be geared, as was Rena's in the discussion above, to what you see and how it relates to the child's experience. For example: "Look at the doll in this ad. Does she look like anyone you know? How is she the same or different from the people we know?" Or, "Look at the two girls in this ad. Do you play like that? Do you look like that?" As children get a little older, you can begin to talk about things like the fairness of only having males or females do certain things or use certain toys—for instance, Rena might have asked her children how they think the female Ghostbuster feels always being left behind, or how they think the male Ghostbusters feel always having to be strong and powerful and whether it's fair to them.

In addition to using this general approach for talking with children about sex-role stereotypes on TV, you can also discuss those you see in movies, on toy boxes, and in real situations. If a discussion ensues, try to follow the child's lead, asking new questions or making comments based on what she has said and using her words for describing things.

♦ **Give children real tasks that allow them to have direct experience with a variety of roles.**

Because children bring their experiences into dramatic play, the broader the range of first-hand experiences they have, the more varied will be the roles they explore in play.

Both girls and boys should have experiences cooking, washing dishes, caring for others, fixing broken things, moving heavy things, playing ball and roughhousing. A boy is more likely to pretend to cook for his family in play if he has had some real cooking experiences. A girl is more likely to assume a strong role in pretend play if she has felt strong and capable in everyday life.

Many parents report that they unconsciously choose certain of their children to participate in specific tasks based on their sex. Here is an interview with one mother:

"I noticed that my husband always picked up the children, especially our son, and swung them up in the air, or over his shoulder. I had never done this, but when we all went on an outing the other day, I grabbed my daughter and slung her over my shoulder and carried her that way . . . It felt very new, but great."

♦ **Present a variety of gender role models to girls and boys.**

Even though media models convey powerful messages about gender roles to children, firsthand experiences in the family, school and community do too. Children will benefit from seeing parents assume a variety of roles at home. Mothers who build and fix things and fathers who perform nurturing roles and cook and bathe children will give children information for the categories they are forming about what women and men do.

We talked to one father who was very conscious of trying to broaden his children's views of gender roles. He brought his children with him on errands where they would see alternate sex role models. He had his car repaired at a garage that employed women mechanics, and chose female doctors and dentists when possible. After a trip to the woman pediatrician, he relayed this conversation which gives an amusing window into young children's dichotomous thinking:

> Howard: Do you like to go to the doctor?
> Jeff: I like Dr. Stavis.
> Howard: Did you know that women can be doctors?
> Jeff: No, only men are doctors.
> Howard: But what about Dr. Stavis; she's a woman.
> Jeff: Dr. Stavis is a nurse.
> Howard: No, Dr. Stavis is a doctor.
> Jeff: Oh, I didn't know.

We know of one kindergarten boy, Ricky, who was unusually outspoken in identifying what boys could and could not do. His teacher's repeated efforts to lure him into activities that went beyond sex stereotypes usually met with failure. Then, one day, when a group of children was about to begin a cooking project which he said he wouldn't do because "boys don't cook," the teacher asked him about the kinds of things his dad did in the kitchen. He said that his dad cooked hot dogs and washed the dishes. The next day she set up the housekeeping area with a pile of plastic dishes and soapy water and asked him to help out like his dad did. Not only did he enthusiastically do the wash-up. He began preparing meals with pretend food so that "there would be more dishes to wash."

Sometimes children can be exposed to information, such as Jeff seeing a female doctor or Ricky seeing his father perform duties in the kitchen, which they do not assimilate. Young children's thinking can be so compartmentalized, they don't always adjust their ideas to what they see. Adults can explicitly point out, as Ricky's teacher and Howard did, things in the child's experience that might go unnoticed or unused.

♦ **Have books available that picture men and women in a variety of roles, and that tell stories about girls and boys doing nonsexist activities.**

Books, like television programs, are an important source of information about gender roles for children to use in their dramatic play. While there are many books that portray girls and boys in a variety of different roles, there are also books which contain subtle, if not blatant sexism.

A quick look at a children's book can let a parent know if it contains sexist messages. Most books published before the early 1970s portrayed males and females in stereotypic ways. Women were seen doing domestic chores, girls playing with dolls, and characters such as the wicked stepmother were common; males, on the other hand, had adventures, confronted and solved problems and were the bastions of physical strength and bravery.

While more recent books are less likely to contain such glaringly sexist images, much subtle sexism still exists. It is important to check the illustrations and ask how they would affect a child's ideas of sex roles and his or her self-image. Also, the language and content of the story can reflect bias as well. Girls are less frequently represented as main characters in books, and often achieve things with the help of males or because of good looks more than ability. The really important deeds are often accomplished by boys. If you decide to read a book to your child that conveys sexist messages (and many of them are worth reading), you can talk about the sexism with your child.

There are wonderful books that portray girls as strong and capable, such as *The Wizard of Oz,* by Frank Baum, and boys as nurturing, such as *William's Doll,* by Charlotte Zolotow. There are also some very fine books that present themes that appeal to the same developmental needs as war play, but which offer less sex-stereotyped models for expressing these needs.

Having homemade and recycled props available for acting out stories will encourage children to extend and deepen the meaning these stories have for them. A few very simple props can excite children's imagination and lead them into creative dramatics. The characters and images they represent offer powerful alternatives to the restrictive gender models offered by the media and toys. The practical ideas section of this book contains many ideas for making props and costumes at home that can contribute to less gender-stereotyped dramatic play.

7
Learning About War, Learning About Peace
The Political Lessons in War Play

I was now embarked on a military career. This orientation was entirely due to my collection of soldiers. I had ultimately nearly fifteen hundred. They were all of one size, all British, and organised as an infantry division with a cavalry brigade. My brother Jack commanded the hostile army . . . The day came when my father himself paid a formal visit of inspection. All the troops were arranged in the correct formation of attack. He spent twenty minutes studying the scene— which was really impressive . . . At the end he asked me if I would like to go into the Army. I thought it would be splendid to command an Army, so I said "Yes" at once: and immediately I was taken at my word . . . the toy soldiers turned the current of my life. Henceforward all my education was directed to passing into Sandhurst [officer training school].
—Winston Churchill, *The Story of My Early Life* (1944, p. 19-20)*

It's Only Pretend (Or Is It?)

Many of the parents we have talked with see their children pretending to shoot and kill with a kind of intensity and apparent pleasure that they find disturbing. They wonder what is happening to the peaceful values they are trying to instill in their children. They worry about the political and moral lessons their children are learning from their war play and ask where this compelling interest might lead. And many who argue for a ban of war play and toys base their argument on the grounds that children learn militaristic attitudes and values from the play.

But adults who advocate allowing war play often dismiss this concern. They argue that war play has different meaning for children than it

---

*Winston Churchill. *A roving commission: The story of my early life*. New York: Charles Scribner's Sons, 1944.

has for adults. For children, they say, it is only pretend and not connected to the violence of the real world. They say that adults should not bring in the realities of violence and war (as Churchill's father did) when they look at their children play.

There is certainly some truth to this argument. Children's political thinking is very different from that of adults. Children have very different ideas about what a country is, what a government is, or what causes fighting between people and countries. This can make it difficult to recognize what children's political ideas are, where the lessons they use to form them come from or how the political ideas used in war play relate to adult ideas and values.

But saying children's war play is only pretend is only part of the truth. For, if the "child is father to the man," then the attitudes and values that we have as adults have their roots in the early years. And, just as Winston Churchill thought his play with his toy soldiers influenced the whole course of his education and adult life, so can war play help establish the roots of the political world of all children.

We saw in Chapter Three ("Bang! Bang! You're Dead!") that the quality of Jake and Owen's war play affected what they learned. But, it is not just the quality of war play that is important when we focus on political learning. It is also the content that children bring from the world around them to their war play that contributes to the political lessons they learn.

Andrew is making his own unique sense of what he's heard about guerilla ("gorilla") war.

Moral and political experiences are part of children's daily lives. They see and experience good and evil, right and wrong, and the disparities in wealth and power among people. They begin to construct their own ideas about politics from an early age, using their everyday experiences as a basis. A child might learn the label "America" to define where she lives, and then hears on the television news that America bombed Libya or provided food to hungry Ethiopians. She may conclude that there are some people "we" want to hurt and some people "we" want to help. She may even connect this to ideas about who are friends and who are enemies. When a child watching an old movie sees Indians attack a group of "peaceful" white settlers and then get killed for their attack, she may begin to think that Indians are bad, the enemy.

Children bring political experiences from daily life into their dramatic play where political meaning is constructed. The ideas to which they have been exposed perform an important role in shaping their play and the learning that results from it. Much of the political content children are bringing to their war play today comes from television and television-related sources. In the world of war toys and war cartoons, antisocial messages about violence, conflict and animosity among people prevail. Children do not see examples of positive social attitudes and interactions they could use to broaden the political content in their play.

One parent's experiences with her son, Hal, provides us with more understanding of how children move back and forth between their real and pretend worlds.

Hal Meets the Russians

When Hal was four and a half I took him to see the animated movie, *An American Tail*. The movie begins as a young mouse, Feival, and his Jewish family are celebrating Chanukah in Russia. (We're Jewish and celebrate Chanukah.) Suddenly evil looking Cossacks, riding on giant black cats, descend on Feival's home and viciously attack the family. The mice miraculously escape and flee to the United States on a boat, but Feival is washed overboard and ends up in a bottle which floats to New York City. During the remainder of the movie, Feival despairingly searches for his family, as he is threatened by one evil character after another. He has an emotional, tear-filled family reunion at the end.

Hal was very scared during most of the movie, climbing on my lap and crying during some scenes. He needed a lot of reassurance from me that the movie was pretend. Afterward he wanted to talk about the "mean Cossacks"—why they were so mean, whether they were real and around today. I kept pointing out that it was pretend and had a happy ending. A real indication of how the movie was affecting Hal came a couple of days later.

Hal took some metallic stickers shaped like snowflakes, paper and a pen. He glued a row of stickers across the top of the paper and said to me, "These look like snowflakes but they're really bombs." He asked me to draw people "running away" along the bottom which I reluctantly did. As I drew, he said, "They're running away from the bombs." He began to draw lines from the bombs to the people, making "Pow" noises, and to scribble over the people and bombs as he passionately called out, "Run fast, the Russians are going to get you! Run fast from the Russians! Run to America." Much of the picture was obliterated, but he got two more pieces of paper and continued with the bomb attack. With more paper, the story gradually progressed until finally the people escaped the bombs and went to a "carnival" in America where they were "safe from the Russian bombs."

Hal's sticker "bombs" falling on the people he asked his mother to draw.

> As things were winding down, Hal suddenly jumped up and got a suitcase from his closet. He packed it with his "gun" (a block) and began running around the house calling out, "Everybody run. Let's get out of Russia. Run to America. Yea, we made it!" For several days, Hal continued to play this story and got his friends to join in too.

Hal is clearly very affected by the movie. As all children would try to do after an intense and upsetting experience, he looks for ways to work through his thoughts and feelings. First, he turns to his mother for reassurance and for help in sorting out fantasy from reality—are Cossacks real? Are they from a long time ago? But conversation is rarely enough for a young child.

Hal turns to "action" drawings, a form of "war play" more common to children older than Hal, but it seems to serve his needs well. The movie is clearly the impetus for the drawings. Some of the most dramatic aspects of the movie are used—Russia and America—as well as the basic sequence of events, but Hal doesn't just imitate the movie. He makes many substitutions—bombs and people and a carnival replace the Cossacks, cats, mice. He brings in important events from his everyday life—a recent snowstorm and a visit to a carnival the previous summer. At the end, once he has created his peaceful and safe world, Hal turns to dramatic play where the themes from the movie and drawings continue to reverberate.

In his own way, Hal is involved in the same kind of active play that Mario and Jake and Owen were in previous chapters. He does a wonderful job using discussions with his mother, as well as his drawings and play to work out his own personal meaning of the movie. As he does this, he is learning some important political lessons. He is learning about "Russia" which he continually associates with the enemy, violence and evil. And he is learning about "America," a place that is peaceful and safe. As is common for children his age, Hal doesn't look for a reason for the bomb attack in Russia. He also doesn't try to find a way to stop the bombing; the only way out is escape to America.

Hal is also learning that he can resolve the story and his own feelings through play. Hal himself changes the violent situation into a peaceful one, and through this process comes to a resolution about the movie and his feelings about it. He creates a story in which people save themselves through their own actions and make a peaceful happy world without ever fighting. This sense of empowerment Hal gains from his play provides him with one of the most important early political lessons children can learn—that they have the power to change things and to resolve them peacefully.

Where Pretend Meets Real

So it is, that through war play, Hal brings some of the movie into his pretend play and learns about both war and peace. But, does his make-believe world influence what he thinks about the real political world? We get some insight into how the political ideas used in play can cross the boundary into reality from the rest of Hal's story:

> The suitcase play gradually disappeared and so did "Russia," but almost a year later Hal got a new babysitter. Eva's family had recently emigrated here from the Soviet Union and she had a strong accent. His first comment to her was, "Why do you talk that way?" When she said she came from Russia, Hal paused, frowned and changed the subject. The next day he asked me why Eva left Russia and kept saying she was a nice babysitter. Then he began talking about the movie—whether the things in the movie were real and when they happened. He began using his suitcase and "Russia" in his war play again.

We don't know whether the Russian babysitter is Hal's first direct exposure to "Russia" as a real place where real people live today. But here is a real Russian who left Russia just like the characters in the movie had done. This coming together of the real and pretend seems to trigger confusion for Hal. He wants to know why Eva left. (Could it be for the same reasons as Feival?) He reassures himself and his mother that he has met a "nice Russian," perhaps because the idea of Russia he developed in his play is that of an evil place with evil people. He again tries to sort out whether the movie was about something real or not. And he chooses to return to his "Feival" war play, perhaps to work out some new resolution after his ideas have been challenged again by the new information the babysitter provides.

If Hal had seen a negative image of Russians and it didn't affect his political ideas, then it wouldn't matter; but we see how Hal formed an image of Russia in his play that he then used to form an impression of his babysitter. This is an example of the complex process by which children get political information from direct experience (in this case a fictional movie), use it in play to develop political ideas and then use these ideas to help interpret reality. Through this constant back and forth movement between the worlds of real and pretend, children gradually build up an understanding of their political world.

Playing for Keeps

Millions of children saw *An American Tail* during the 1986 Christmas holiday season. Millions more have seen it since as a home video movie. In the spring of 1988 it was still the second most popular home video for children. The process Hal went through here is by no means guaranteed to all children who saw the movie. There are many hazards which can interfere. If children aren't able to ask their parents the kinds of questions Hal asks his mother, then it will be harder to sort out fantasy from reality. If their parents don't allow war play and try to stop it, they won't have an opportunity to work through their thoughts and feelings in the way Hal did. If, instead of coming up with their own unique approaches to play as Hal did, they get toys which are linked to the movie, then they will be channeled into imitating the political messages and violence they have seen. And, if they don't have a chance to meet a Russian babysitter (and how many children do?), who will help them to challenge the unidimensional image of "Russia" conveyed by the movie?

Given how frightening *An American Tail* was for Hal, it was crucial that he had the opportunity to work out his thoughts and feelings through his play. But even if we can help children develop the kind of dramatic play that Hal achieved, is this enough given the political messages which inundate them? Today, much of the political content children are exposed to is much more explicit, violent and overtly propagandistic than what Hal saw in *An American Tail*. We need look no further than the description on a pamphlet in the toy box of one of the best selling toy lines in the United States, GI Joe, to see this:

G.I. Joe® is gearing up for the most massive land, sea and air operation ever!

"Men, as you know, the Cobra forces have grown and now threaten the entire globe. Their evil presence throughout the free world has become a blow against democracy. No matter where you are stationed, your knowledge of your local terrain makes you a valuable part of this campaign to help eliminate Cobra commandos and agents everywhere. We are faced with a major challenge: The enemy is better equipped than ever. The stakes are high. We must coordinate all our combat efforts to eliminate this threat to the American way. All units are ordered to gear up for this international conflict and work as one massive strike force to repel the Cobra menaces from our borders, from our tropical shores to our frozen fields to our big cities. Your training and knowledge of G.I. Joe weapon systems and equipment are urgently needed for Operation: A.C.T.I.O.N."

Hawk

Brigadier General
Commander G.I. Joe Forces

This is a description of a political world created for children by adults. No child would be able to invent such a world for his own war play. Terms like "democracy," "international conflict" and the "free world" can have little meaning to someone who may have only begun to learn that countries exist at all, much less understand warring systems of government. Still, the political messages that this brochure gives to children are quite clear. A child receiving the toy needs to become a part of the battle; his help is vital if his world is to remain safe. He must fight and protect the world with the new toy or he will be letting his country down. These instructions leave little room for anything but fighting. The single-purpose toy in the box ensures that his attention will stay on performing his role and on violence. If he still has any doubts, he can become an "Official Joe" by joining the "GI Joe Club" which is also described in the brochure. He can also turn on the TV set and get more explicit instructions to guide his play from daily episodes of the "GI Joe" cartoon.

GI Joe is only one of the many TV cartoons with accompanying toy lines that provide children with violent material for war play. Each program has slightly different settings, characters and twists, but the underlying structure, plot and political messages of all the shows are basically the same. "Masters of the Universe" takes place in space, whereas "GI Joe" occurs on earth. "Transformers" are all robots and machines, while "Joes and Cobras" are humans. "Dinoriders" are from billions of years in the past and "Captain Power" (the first program to use guns that can interact with the TV set) takes place in the future after the Earth as we know it has been destroyed by nuclear war.

Despite these superficial differences, the underlying political messages are remarkably similar. The "good guys" (wherever they live) are threatened by the "bad guys" for a reason which is unstated. They must protect themselves with weapons and a readiness for battle, which can occur at any time. Fighting is glamorized because the real pain that results from it is not shown. No solution other than fighting is ever considered. And despite the unending and ruthless efforts of the "bad guys," the "good guys" always win in the end.

Another common feature is the narrow definition of the characters. They are unidimensional in their total goodness or badness. Their actions are a result of their being defined as good or bad. They spend most of their time fighting. They do not have lives or personality traits which children can identify with outside of the fighting. Physical strength, power and bravery are the most valued human traits.

There is also rigid stereotyping of the characters. As we described in Chapter Six ("Whatever Happened to Annie Oakley?"), it is a male world; females rarely appear and when they do they are usually in need of rescue. It's also a world where the "enemy" is dehumanized—with foreign sounding voices, covered faces—where anything "not like me" is threatening. And there are racial stereotypes—the "bad guys" often wear black, have black hair and the "good guys" have light hair, colorful clothing and caucasian features.

GI Joe Has Got to Go

Every society provides its children with political information which forms the foundation for an understanding of war and peace. In the United States today, much of this information is coming from sources other than parents and the home, and much of it is militaristic.

For children growing up in the current political climate and using their war play to develop views of war and peace, there is a two-pronged challenge. First, probably now more than ever before, they need to achieve the quality of play which will help them construct their own meaning of the ideas which bombard them. For without a lot of high quality play, children will run the risk of just mimicking the messages they hear without ever establishing a foundation for their own political ideas which can expand and develop over time.

Second, children will need to be confronted with ideas and experiences which challenge the simplistic and violent political themes in their play. For without this challenge, they can easily remain stuck with the militaristic thinking promoted by media and toys.

The adults who care about children have a crucial role to play in helping children meet both of these challenges. We have already discussed in Chapter Three how parents can meet the first challenge— help meaningful war play develop. To meet the second challenge, parents may need to think and act more deliberately in the political socialization of their children in order to counteract the influences from media and toys.

GUIDE
Encouraging Prosocial Values
and Attitudes

Given that children's play is filled with violence, we need to know how parents can influence the political lessons their children learn through play. Even though negative political messages have gained influence over many young children today, there are ways to counteract them. You can try to influence the political ideas that are part of play itself as well as create a broader context in which children can learn prosocial behavior and values. These guidelines can strengthen the part you play in the political socialization of your own children, a role which many parents today are trying to actively reclaim.

◆ **Learn about your child's social and political ideas and what they mean to him.**

Because the content of war play has different meaning for children than it does for us, you will need to try to figure out your child's meanings before you can effectively influence his ideas. A lot can be learned about a child's political thinking by observing his war play. What are the allies and enemies like, what do they fight over, who wins and how? What kinds of stereotypes appear—about males and females, different ethnic or racial groups, other countries? Is "real world" terminology used? What connections does it have with real events? Are all conflicts resolved by violence?

You can ask questions to learn more about your child's ideas. While talking cannot be a substitute for watching, there are times when a careful question can provide valuable insights into the meaning a child's war play world has for him. Some questions work better than others. A question such as, "What is the enemy's name?" has only one answer and leaves little room for a child's ideas to come through. But, a more open-ended one such as, "Who is this bad guy you're shooting? Tell me about him," might help you learn more about what your child thinks. The exact questions you ask will have to grow out of the play you observe. And, as we have said, there is the risk of intruding too much. Often, it will be better to ask questions about the meaning of play at a later time, when it is no longer going on.

◆ **Try to influence the political ideas used in play that are learned from media, toys and friends.**

As we discussed in Chapter Three ("Bang! Bang! You're Dead!: Why War Play?"), getting children's war play beyond merely imitating violence is an important step in helping them use their play to meet their needs. In addition, because play is a primary way children work out their political ideas, helping them expand their war play is one of the most effective ways we have of influencing the political ideas they learn.

In the following example, Lucy uses an approach to expand her son's war play that we have discussed before; but here she also is trying to influence his political ideas:

> Jethro would rather play GI Joe than anything else. He sits with his action figures and crashes them into each other over and over again, making "Pow! Pow!" noises. He does this same thing day after day. Lucy gets a box, some glue, markers and paper. She asks Jethro, "Can you make a place where Joe can hide from Cobra (his enemy)?"

The idea catches on. Jethro works on the box for a long time, then starts to use it with his GI Joe and Cobra dolls. Later that week, when Joe and Cobra are in an intense battle again, Lucy says, "Oh, I think Cobra is hurt. Can you build a hospital for him?" She puts some small blocks out. Jethro starts building, and they have the following conversation:

Lucy: Tell me about Cobra.
Jethro: He's GI Joe's enemy.
Lucy: What else?
Jethro: He's just the enemy. He's bad.
Lucy [Getting out paper and markers as his play winds down]: Does Cobra have a family? Can you draw them? Does he have children? Do they think he's bad?
Lucy [a few minutes later after Jethro has completed his drawing]: Do you think Cobra would like a nice bubble bath? He must be tired. Do you think he likes bubbles as much as you do?

First, Lucy tries to find out about Jethro's play by watching and asking him questions about it. Then she tries some things that grow out of what he is doing and thinking. She makes suggestions to expand the violent focus of his play. She offers him materials that give him an idea for a less violent story—a box for making a hiding place for Joe. She also suggests that he build a hospital where Cobra can go when he's hurt. In the end she tries to develop his ideas further as his play ends.

Lucy's efforts help Jethro expand his concept of the enemy and his understanding of the effects of violence. At the beginning Jethro's idea of Cobra is that he is all bad; all he does is fight. He doesn't think about Cobra as a character with feelings or needs, or about what happens to him when Joe attacks. In the course of the play, Jethro begins to think more about how Cobra might get hurt from the fighting, and that he too may need help. Jethro is learning that enemies can be human and have many of the same needs he has. Lucy furthers these growing understandings when she relates an activity that Jethro loves (bubble baths) to Cobra—maybe Cobra likes bubble baths, too; maybe he has feelings and feels pleasure just like Jethro does.

Lucy uses Jethro's war play to help his political ideas develop beyond the stereotypes he's seen in media characters. She makes many tiny, incremental efforts. Not all will be of interest to Jethro. But over time, they will have a positive, cumulative effect.

There are also times when you can talk about the political ideas in your child's play when they're not directly tied to a play episode. When you do this, still try to choose some concrete focus for the discussion. For instance, point to a picture of a "good guy" character on a toy box (the ones with huge muscles and angry faces) and ask, "How can we tell this guy is good?" Ask how your child thinks Cobra got to be so bad and mean; or if he thinks the "bad guys" ever kiss anybody, or why he thinks their voices sound the way they do. Or you can talk about how GI Joe might try to solve his problems without fighting.

In such conversations, it is often easier to express your own ideas and feelings—as long as you stay concrete and at your child's level. Try comments like, "I'm sure glad that real men are not like Cobra," "I do wish GI Joe and Cobra would find a way to stop fighting—a way they could make peace. I can't stand it that they always have to fight. Do you think they can ever be friends?"

You can also try to provide your child with direct experiences that counteract some of the political content he's using. If he's using Russians as enemies in his play (which could come from the GI Joe TV show), you can help develop a more humanized view of the Soviet Union—by reading Soviet fairy tales or pointing out Russian folk toys (like little wooden nesting dolls) when the opportunity arises. Sometimes a simple piece of information which contradicts a stereotype can be useful, for example, "You always say black is for the 'bad guy'; so am I a bad Mom when I wear my black dress?"

♦ **Try to limit exposure to violent images and single-purpose war toys for as long as you can.**

Earlier in this chapter we saw how Hal used his experience with pretend play and open-ended materials to come to terms with his reaction to the movie, *An American Tail*. His well-developed play repertoire had a great deal to do with how well he could resolve the experience and what he learned from it. The more time that children have to develop a broad play repertoire before the onslaught of war toys and violent TV begins, the more tools they will have to counteract their negative effects later on.

Once children begin to be exposed to violence, they will need to work through what they have seen as Hal did. But the less violence they see, and the more tools they have as players, the greater will be their ability to withstand the threat that exposure to violence poses for them.

Finding effective ways to limit your child's exposure may not be easy; many parents are disturbed to discover how little control they have. But you can carefully select the movies your child sees, avoid trips to stores you know are full of war toys, ask adults who give your child gifts to steer away from war toys, and let relatives and friends know how you are trying to limit exposure to violence. There are also suggestions in the guideline sections of Chapter Four ("From Sticks and Stones to Lasers") and Five ("Mama Won't You Buy Me a GI Joe?") which will help you limit early exposure to war toys.

Many parents have also successfully limited their children's exposure to television violence. Those who are successful usually find that the keys to success are good planning, creativity, patience and flexibility, as well as developing a good sense of what is right for their particular family. Some of the approaches they have tried include: not having a TV during their child's first few years; trying to delay regular TV viewing as long as possible; trying not to watch much TV themselves while their children are around; and, using a VCR and videotapes as an alternative to regular television. If you videotape programs for later viewing, ads can be edited out. In addition, moving the TV to a room (like a bedroom) that is not the focal point of family life can help keep it out of children's minds. Putting the TV on a cart with wheels, so that it can get pushed into a corner after each use, can also accomplish this.

◆ **Talk with children about the content of television.**
Once exposure to violent television programs does begin, parents have an important role to play. For a variety of legitimate reasons, many parents avoid watching their children's favorite TV shows. But it is important that you sometimes watch shows together and discuss them, starting with open-ended questions, and trying to let the child's ideas lead the discussion. And when you don't watch, ask what happened on the shows that she watched, and discuss them as much as possible.

Children can learn to talk about the ideas and values on TV shows when conversations are geared to how they are thinking and making sense of things. For example, rather than moralizing about entertainment violence with a remark such as, "He-Man is a terrible show; there's too much violence," it's often better to ask, "Why do you think He-Man solves all of his problems by fighting?" or, "How do you think He-Man feels when he punches that guy?" When we make remarks like the former, children easily "tune out"; the words don't seem to connect to how they see things. But the latter questions would capture many children's interest. They could help children to think about familiar ideas in new ways. Using disequilibrium like this to promote critical thinking about television will gradually help children learn to evaluate shows for themselves.

You can use this approach to raise questions or make comments about any aspect of television content: violence, conflict resolution, images of enemies, racism and sexism. The tricky part is remembering to begin with how the child is understanding these issues, and then pose questions that relate to that understanding.

◆ **Set limits on the television your child watches, but be willing to negotiate.**

Once your child discovers all of the programs offered on television for children, you will be in for a challenge. Parents draw the line on TV in many different places, but unless you decide to have no restrictions at all, you'll have to figure out what limits to have and how to set them. Whatever you decide, try to explain the reasons for your limits (this often means explaining your values to your child) in terms a child can understand ("I don't like that show because they fight every time they have a problem. They don't talk things over the way we try to").

In the following conversation, Vincent wants his son Nate to watch less television and have more time to play. Nate, who has recently discovered several new shows, wants to watch all the time.

> Vincent: Look at today. You woke up, watched "Sesame Street," then "Mr. Rogers," and went to school. When you got home from Raymond's, you watched "He-Man," and then had dinner. Now you're watching "Square One TV." This is the first day that you haven't played with one toy. I haven't played with you, and I really miss that. It's okay to see the shows that you saw, but it's just too much TV when there's so little time at home. If you want to see "Square One," then there has to be no "He Man."
> Nate: No, I like "He-Man" better. But can I just see the end of the mystery on "Square One?" That's the best.
> Vincent: You mean, tomorrow night, we'll finish dinner, play, then turn on the TV to only see the end of "Square One"?
> Nate: Yes.
> Vincent: I think that's okay. Let's try it.

Vincent explains the problem to Nate in very specific terms; he lists the events in Nate's day one after the other in sequence. He tells Nate that he is watching too much TV, and explains *why* it is too much by listing the things that Nate is missing out on. He shares how he feels with Nate, how he misses having their play time together.

Vincent poses a problem to Nate and a solution (that Nate give up watching "He-Man" in the afternoons), but he is willing to negotiate. Nate accepts the problem but suggests a different solution (he'd rather watch "He-Man," but wants to see the very end of "Square One," too.) Vincent shows Nate how his solution will work in practice (by applying it to tomorrow night's events). Nate still has room to back out, but when he agrees, he is committed. Together Vincent and Nate have devised a plan that they both think can work.

No matter where you want to draw the line on television watching, you can use a process like this one. In putting it into practice, you are teaching powerful political lessons to your child about how to negotiate and share in decision-making. Children can participate in dialogues such as this one from an early age if we help by talking in terms they can understand. And over time, they will learn to take on more of the control themselves.

♦ **Make the job of controlling TV as predictable as possible.**

There are a few techniques that can help to reduce the tension that parents often have with their young children over watching television. They all involve setting up predictable routines, something few young children can do without adult assistance.

The most important thing of all is to plan ahead because it helps children to take control of their own TV viewing and manage it on their own. Children will need help in understanding what's offered on television, choosing shows to watch, and seeing how they fit with the rules of the house (e.g., "You can watch one hour of TV a day. Let's figure out which shows you like and try to choose what you will watch this week"). Vincent and Nate succeeded in planning ahead when a problem arose, which is often the way planning ahead begins.

Go through the TV listings with your child and discuss options. This gives her a chance to reflect on shows and discuss them with you at a time when they are not actually on. Once they are on, it is not the time to set limits. A parent who turns off a program that is in progress can leave a child feeling powerless and angry.

Write down with your child, in a form that she can read (pictures, dictated words, her own written words), the shows that she decides to watch. Put this information in a prominent place that she can refer to on her own.

Make your own limits clear. But leave room for your child to have some choice, and make it clear what can and cannot be negotiated—for instance, "You can watch one 'fighting' cartoon a week; it can be any one that you want." With younger children, the choices will have to be simpler—such as, "You can watch 'Care Bears' or 'Smurfs.' Which one would you like to see?"

♦ **Help children experience cooperation and interdependence at home.**

Children learn a great many political lessons at home—about power and authority, values, right and wrong. These lessons take on special significance at a time when there are important lessons emanating from agents outside of the home as well. Parents wishing to counteract the effects on children of exposure to violence may want to think in a deliberate way about how to provide a home context that teaches cooperation and peace.

Violence is often visible, and dramatic. Therefore, it is usually more comprehensible to children than concepts of cooperation and peace, which are more abstract and harder to see. Learning to cooperate with others is a slow process for children. Gradually they learn to see how what they do relates to others, how what they do affects others and how the part everyone plays can connect to a whole activity. But it takes a long time and a lot of direct experience.

An effective way to help children construct an understanding of cooperation and interdependence is to help them play a meaningful role in ongoing family routines. For example, a young child putting dishes out on the table for dinner can see that this is one important part of preparation for the family meal. Because it is hard for children to grasp part/whole relationships, parents can point out the overall goal, such as having dinner, and how the child's part helped others and the system to work as a whole. Participating in appropriate ways in such tasks as cooking, gardening and shopping can provide children with the concrete experience of contributing to a family system.

Children can also learn how to help family members in authentic ways. An older sibling can help to make a costume for a younger child who loves to role play, or to help in taking care of a baby. A younger child can make a book for an older sibling or help her clean up her room. There are also many ways children can be helped to think of special things to do for friends (make cards when they are sick, lend them a toy).

Real life situations offer many opportunities for learning to solve problems in nonviolent ways. Starting at an early age, children can begin to participate in solving all kinds of everyday problems using the same kind of model suggested for resolving conflicts that arise in play at the end of Chapter Three. There are endless situations that brew in every family that can become an opportunity to work on cooperative problem solving—for instance, "It's hot tonight and Joey and Rita both want the fan in their room. What can we do?"; or, "Darren wants to watch 'Transformers' and his father wants the news. How can we handle this?" When everyone involved jointly works out a solution, and when solutions are examined for their effects on everyone, children are learning political values as well as creative, noncoercive problem-solving skills.

There are also many ways to minimize competition at home. Young children will feel less competitive with siblings if there are predictable systems which allow them to see that their needs will be met. Such systems can pertain to many different issues—from time with parents ("My father reads me a book every other day"), to materials ("This playdough is for all three of us to share"). Games that have winners and losers can foster competition. There are some excellent cooperative games that get children to work together toward a common goal. (See Chapter Twelve—"Resources and Organizations.")

♦ **Help children feel a sense of empowerment in their lives.**
Children need to know that they can make a difference in their world and they need to learn how to do it. This is one of the most important political lessons we can teach them. One way that children's sense of empowerment is being undermined today is in their play, where they have often given up contol to toys and other influences. By helping your children regain control of their play (in the ways discussed throughout this book), you are making an important contribution to their political development.

We have also already discussed many ways that you can help your children feel empowered in their relationships with others and in the home—empowered to express their ideas and have them be heard, to play a role in influencing decisions that affect them, to know how to solve problems with others that take everyone's needs and desires into account.

There are also concrete ways that young children can begin to learn to take action to affect the world beyond the home. When your child has a complaint or point of view about something, help her find a way to express it. In the last chapter, we discussed ways of helping your child take action around consumer problems. A similar approach can work with other problems. For instance, if the neighborhood playground has too much broken glass, write a letter of complaint together to the mayor or try to organize a neighborhood clean-up. When choosing which complaints to pursue, pick ones that are likely to yield results, so your child sees that actions like this can have an effect.

Finally, many kinds of political action that adults take part in are great for young children too, because they can *see* what is happening and participate—for example, in rallies, fund-raising walks, and leafletting. Efforts like these help children feel you have a role to play in affecting their world and that there are alternatives to violence in trying to bring about change.

8
Calling the Shots
Public Policy and War Play

The effects of the expansion of the war toy industry in the eighties have been felt by more than just parents and children in the United States. At the annual International Toy and Hobby Fair held in London in January, 1987, US war toys were among the most prominently featured items. This fair, aimed at European and Asian toy buyers, is a primary way that the latest toys reach countries outside of the US. All of the major American toy manufacturers were present, many with elaborate enclosed display areas as large as a good-sized house.

Among the most dramatic war toy "exhibits" was Lazer Tag by Mattell. Male models dressed in silver lamé space suits went around the huge exhibit hall shooting at each other with Lazer Tag weapons and every hour they performed a special demonstration, complete with smoke and sound effects, in a glass-enclosed room at the Mattell exhibit area. At the Coleco exhibit, one of the items prominently displayed in the Rambo toy line was a pair of action figures—Arab, Nomad twins, the "good" one dressed in white and the "evil" one dressed in black—which had been taken off the US market a few months earlier because of public protest over the racist and stereotyped nature of the twins. At many of the US war toy exhibits, TV monitors loudly broadcasted the cartoon programs and TV advertisements which went with the toy lines.

But while US television and toy businesses devote energy to finding new markets around the world, there are other forces at work in the international arena as well. Several transnational and international organizations, such as the European Youth Conference, the European Parliament, the Nordic Council, the World Congress on Youth and UNESCO at the United Nations, have discussed concerns over war toys, and in some cases have passed resolutions condemning them.

Making a Choice

Individual countries have taken a variety of approaches to the marketing of violence to children, as well as to the play environment of which war toys are a part. What happens in the United States is only one example; different countries go about creating play environments for children in very different ways. In Sweden, for example, consideration of children's play environments occurs at a national level, and responsibility for creating a healthy play culture is shared among government, business and parents. Within this overall context, a voluntary agreement to eliminate the advertising and sale of war toys (depicting modern warfare from 1914 onward) has been reached by the National Board for Consumer Policies, the Swedish Council for Children's Play and the toy trade organizations. Finland has taken an approach similar to Sweden; on October 2, 1986, an agreement was signed by the National Board for Social Welfare and the Entrepreneurs for Toy and Hobby Equipment Manufacturing to refrain from the manufacture, import and sale of war toys. Norway has a similar voluntary agreement.

But while we see these examples from other countries, in the United States there has been little public dialogue about the quality of the play culture we should provide for children or the role war toys should have within it. Political and economic forces work against having such a dialogue. There is a current belief in the US which favors limiting the role of government in people's lives and the marketplace and preserving the rights of the individual. Many argue that it would be very difficult, if not undesirable, to try to achieve a consensus here concerning what a healthy play environment should look like; our society is so diverse that people would define this play environment in many very different ways.

These forces, strengthened during the Reagan years, have led to the belief that the bulk of the burden to create a healthy play environment belongs to parents. But for parents today, this is a misplaced burden, an unattainable task. The responsibility for creating this environment should be shared by all members of adult society and their community and institutions, including government.

Pulling the Rug Out

In the minds of many parents we interviewed, who are working to limit their children's exposure to violence, the responsibility for the gratuitous violence in the play environment lies with the television and toy industries. Yet industry representatives say they are simply producing what sells. But given our economic system, this is only half of the equation. For the way toy manufacturers maximize sales and profits is by creating demand for their products through marketing.

Toy makers and television producers usually counter the accusations made against them with the rejoinder that parents have a choice. If they would only monitor their children's TV viewing and have the courage to say "no" to TV and toys, there would be no problem. But as we have seen over and over again, most parents have difficulty exercising this control in the current social climate; and, as we've argued in this book, trying to exercize this kind of control is not necessarily an appropriate goal in the current context.

As all this buck passing goes on, the blame (and responsibility) is rarely placed where it belongs. Since the 1930s, we have had federal regulatory agencies in the United States whose job it is to protect the public from abuses which might occur in the marketplace. The Federal Communications Commission was created in 1934 to intervene in cases where the marketplace, if left unattended, would lead to socially ill effects. Throughout the 1960s and 1970s, the FCC adopted many regulations designed to protect children from a variety of abuses and forms of commercial exploitation.

But in the 1980s, Ronald Reagan came to office championing the rights of the individual and a "hands-off" government. He advocated a reduced role for government especially in the marketplace, and deregulation of the broadcasting industry. His FCC chairman, Mark Fowler, calling the television just another "appliance" with pictures, declared that the marketplace would determine the public interest. Methodically, the FCC under Fowler set about dismantling the regulations which had accumulated for the two previous decades.

As government withdrew from its protective role, whatever balance had existed among parents, government and the TV/toy industries was profoundly disrupted. This imbalance allowed manufacturers to move in and profit while children and families paid the costs (the very situation the FCC was created to prevent). In this new equation, parents have been edged out. They have lost much of their previous control over their children's play culture. And the diversity which had previously characterized the play of American children has been undermined as play has become dominated by nationally advertised toys and media which fostered the same kind of play for *all* children (although different for girls than for boys).

We were left with and have inherited a situation where manufacturers have become, in a disturbingly real sense, caretakers of the nation's children. They have been allowed to assume, without public dialogue or debate, a growing influence over children's play, thoughts, and desires, an influence which is, for the most part, a negative one; for these caretakers do not base their decisions on the well-being of children but on the well-being of their profits. And if violence sells, then they provide it, no matter what the costs are to children and society, no matter how much the values they push conflict with those of families. In this situation, children have been unable to protect themselves from the seductive influences of these pseudocaretakers. And parents, who would never voluntarily choose caretakers who did not put their children's interests first, have been unable to prevent the shift that has occurred or to protect their children from it.

In the last few years, efforts have been made to pass legislation that would reinstate some or all of the FCC regulations for children's television. And there has been growing support in and out of Congress for such action. The Children's Television Act of 1988 finally did get through Congress with strong bipartisan support only to be vetoed by President Reagan as the last veto of his presidency. The bill called for a minimal reduction in advertising minutes on children's television (still more than pre-deregulation days) and required broadcasters to offer some educational programming for children (also a pre-deregulation requirement). Efforts to reintroduce the bill and put it into law continue.

Whose Rights? Whose Responsibility?

For many citizens who had watched the erosion of social programs which served the needs of children in the eighties, the veto of the Children's Television Act of 1988 was a final legacy of Reagan's policies to the children of America. It is a legacy which some have called "ideological child abuse." Those who have supported deregulation have used the First Amendment and "freedom of expression" as justification. This argument, along with the "free market" argument have consistently been used to rationalize the FCC's withdrawal from regulation of children's broadcasting. Both of these arguments rest on fundamentally flawed assumptions.

First, the basic argument of "free speech" is fallacious when it is applied to children. The right of free speech is guided by the philosophical principle that the public is best served by the free expression of ideas. But where children are concerned, other principles can be injured when free speech is fully exercised. We all know that children are not like adults, that they sometimes need protection from adults who say and do things that are injurious to them. No one would argue that any adult, especially one a child and family does not know, has the right to say whatever he or she pleases to a child. We have seen in this book what happens when adults whose first interest is the profit motive are given this unlimited freedom. So, there are cases, at least where children are concerned, when the public is not best served by unlimited free speech.

In addition, the government has a longstanding tradition of viewing children as different from adults in the legislative and legal systems. There has been a special relationship between children and government in which the government has performed a protective function. There are ample precedents for arguing that the government has not only the right, but the obligation to protect children from abuses in society over which they are unable to protect themselves.

Further, the First Amendment argument is being unfairly applied in the current situation with children's TV and toys, because the free expression of ideas is protected for manufacturers, but *not* for children. Manufacturers and programmers are free to say anything they want as often as they want to say it, but what of the free expression of children's ideas? Haven't we seen in this book that children's creativity, concepts, and imagination are severely impeded by the unrestricted free expression of the ideas of manufacturers?

The second major justification for deregulation is that the marketplace should determine the public interest; and it is fallacious for the same reason as the free speech argument—because we are talking about children. The marketplace argument assumes that children can function in an equal and reciprocal relationship with producers of products. It assumes that consumers, by making informed decisions about the ads they see and about what they buy, have a voice in determining what is placed on the market, and that manufacturers, in their desire to increase profits, respond by producing for the public what it wants. All of this requires that the people who do the consuming have the freedom to choose. And from everything we have seen, when it comes to children, none of these requirements are met.

Because of their developmental vulnerabilities, children certainly cannot have a reciprocal and equal relationship with manufacturers; they cannot make informed decisions about advertisements or purchases nor do they have freedom of choice. Because of how they think, children's minds are made up as soon as they see flashy advertisements or TV programs connected to toys. They cannot possibly compete with the media and marketing experts, whose sole motivation is to get them to think they need something and then, to induce their parents to buy it.

Every Child's Right to Play

Throughout this book, we have taken the point of view of children as we examined the social forces affecting their war play today. Up until now we have focused on how to raise children in the way that is best for them given the current situation. And in this context, we have argued that the best we can do is hold the line on single-purpose war toys where possible, help children make their war play their own as much as possible, and then try to influence the attitudes and values they are learning from their play. Now, it is time to consider what is really best for children—and by so doing, what is best for society.

In 1959, the United Nations adopted the "Rights of the Child," which included a "full opportunity to play" as one basic right of childhood. An assumption underlying this document is that children are a special class of human being, needing special protection and nurturance and that we do not apply the same standards to them that we do to ourselves.

Providing every child with a "full opportunity to play" means first providing basic economic and social supports which are prerequisites for healthy play. Beyond that, it also means providing an environment in which children have the psychic freedom to construct their own dramas built out of their own interpretations of reality. Throughout this book we have tried to show why this is so basic and essential to human development.

Most children in the United States today, despite our best efforts, are not ensured of the "full opportunity to play," and we are a long way from providing it for them. By manipulating and socializing children into violent play, social forces have all but taken away that right.

Following from everything we have said, the full right to play, including the right to engage in war play, would much more likely be assured if there were no violence on children's television, no toys linked to television shows, and no advertising aimed at children. Further, children and their play would be better off if war toys were to disappear completely from toy store shelves. Then, the overemphasis and distortion of war play which results from war toys would disappear, while the opportunity for war play—which many children need and will need as long as they live in a world where they see violence—would be restored.

Bold and comprehensive regulation of children's television and a national ban on war toys would go a long way toward ensuring children of this basic right. Granted, this proposal seems almost absurd in the current political climate. But that is only because none of the public policy arguments regarding children's play have been based on the needs of children. This is not an extreme idea when we understand children, how they think and learn, and their needs—when we can put our own adult ideas and ideology aside long enough to see what would be best for them.

For A Blessed Christmas, You Need A Battery That Can Keep Up With A Holy Terror.

Our Leather Furniture is Built To Stand Up Against A Small Army!

The 'ROMA' Leather Sofa!

SAVE* $500!

$699

$1199 Value*

Imported Italian glove-soft Leather Sofa in bone with durable double-layer back and thick seat cushions.

SAVE* $1596!

$1699

COMPLETE!
3 Piece Set!
Sofa, Loveseat & Chair

We are a long way from taking the public policy steps needed to protect children from socialization into violence.

Many people have argued that before we can enact public policies to curb violence we need conclusive research which proves the link between exposure to media violence and antisocial behavior and attitudes. But the truth is, there are a great many studies resulting from thirty years of research that have already yielded very consistent results. The research has been found persuasive by many important groups, including the National Institute of Mental Health, the American Psychological Association, and US surgeon generals under both Democratic and Republican presidents. The American Academy of Pediatrics spoke out in 1985: "Repeated exposure to televised violence promotes a proclivity to violence and a passive response to its practice." US Senator Paul Simon of Illinois has declared that the evidence that televised violence contributes to aggressive behavior is overwhelming, and has led social scientists as close as they can come to a consensus. In recent Senate testimony, Aletha C. Huston, codirector of the Center for Research on the Influence of Television on Children at the University of Kansas, declared that except for a few studies financed by the television industry, all of the laboratory studies found evidence that televised violence leads to aggressive behavior.

Still, some people continue to say that more conclusive evidence is needed, while they interpret the existing findings according to their own point of view. Bill Johnson, deputy chief of the FCC's media bureau, looks at the same research and says that there is nothing there that says these shows scar kids for life. But the kind of longitudinal research that might prove they do is impossible to conduct reliably; all the variables that influence violent behavior could never be adequately controlled.

The question of war toys and children's television violence is not one that can be decided on the basis of research alone. We already know enough about how and what children learn through play from child development theory and research to draw conclusions now. Until 1984, the FCC did not even feel it was necessary to have established research findings to take a stand on what was healthy for children in order to set policies. Even without any research to rely on, does anyone really think it's a good idea to bombard young children with daily doses of violent entertainment and toys? Does anyone seriously believe that it is of no negative consequence to show violence in large doses to young children? And, can anyone think that society will not pay a price for over-exposing children to violence in their early years? These questions are basic enough to be answered by pure common sense.

Children's Needs and Society's Future

We have tried to show in this book how serious a problem the marketing of violence to children has become for them and for society. The price children pay now for our failure to meet their needs will ultimately be paid by everyone. We live at a time in history when the survival of the globe will depend on people's ability to resolve their differences through nonviolent means; when creativity and imagination will be the main ingredients needed in the search for solutions to global problems.

If public policy were guided by what is in children's best interest (and this is the moral obligation we have to them), then it would be much easier to move toward creating the kinds of national practices and policies they deserve, and much easier to see clearly the path which leads to a healthier play environment for *all* children. The best play environment we can offer to children will also best equip them to live up to the tremendous responsibility they will inherit for finding ways to achieve greater world harmony.

GUIDE
Taking Action

The fact that government has yet to live up to its responsibility to care for and to protect our nation's children should not give us the sense that nothing can be done outside the home now to work against the militarization of childhood. Local government officials, state and federal legislators, community groups, professional and parent organizations, schools and individuals have taken steps to limit the impact of deregulation and to force a change. We have collected endless examples of creative steps, large and small, taken by people at every level of society acting as individuals and as members of organized groups. The few sketched below suggest the range of what is possible.

◆ **There are national organizations that are working against the sale and manufacture of war toys and for less violent and commercialized children's TV.**
—The War Resisters League organized the "Stop War Toys Campaign" in the summer of 1985. Having grown in scope and impact each year, it is probably the best-known effort in the country. The Campaign produces an information and resource packet which includes a wide range of literature intended to educate the public about the dangers of the buildup of war toys. It also serves as a clearinghouse for the activities of grassroots antiwar toy groups across the country. Among its most successful undertakings has been the boycott it has organized against Hasbro's GI Joe toy line, and its annual national petition drive against the manufacturing and sale of war toys. The petitions have been delivered to toy manufacturers each February at the International Toy and Hobby Fair in New York City.

—Action for Children's Television is a nonprofit child advocacy organization focused on encouraging diversity in children's television and truth in TV advertising directed at children. In recent years, it has actively worked to support legislation that would reinstate the FCC's children's television guidelines elimitated in the eighties. It has also been working to educate the public about the problems that have been created by deregulation and has produced useful educational books and videotapes toward this end.

◆ **At the national level, there have been petition drives, letter-writing campaigns, boycotts and legislative initiatives to accomplish such goals as limiting the sale of particular war toys, reregulating children's TV and limiting violent children's television programming.**
—The Association for Childhood Education International, a professional organization of thousands of educators, adopted this statement at its annual 1988 business meeting:

> Whereas the FCC Deregulation of Children's Commercial Television has resulted in inappropriate programming for children, and Whereas Commercial Television Producers are exploiting children through overcommercialization of television, and whereas educational television has been reduced,
> Therefore be it resolved that ACEI state its support of those federal bills which require the FCC to initiate rulemaking proceedings to prescribe standards applicable to commercial television with respect to advertising and require elimination of toy-based and tie-in practices involving the use of program characters to promote products . . .

ACEI continues to keep its membership informed about the status of government action and what members can do to support the resolution.
—The state of Maine introduced legislation in 1988 that would have required the following warning label to be put on all war toys: "WARNING: THINK BEFORE YOU BUY. THIS IS A WAR TOY. PLAYING WITH IT INCREASES ANGER AND VIOLENCE IN CHILDREN. IS THIS WHAT YOU REALLY WANT FOR YOUR CHILD?" The bill didn't pass, but it stimulated a great deal of public dialogue about war toys in Maine and led to the Maine legislature passing a resolution urging Congress to address the issue on a national level.
—Laws were passed in at least a dozen major cities, including Chicago, San Francisco and Detroit, banning the sale and manufacture of realistic toy guns after three separate accidental deaths by police of young men playing with realistic toy guns. The state of California has passed a similar ban. Such efforts have led Toys R Us, the largest toy store chain in the country and the trendsetter for toy manufacturers, to send

word out to manufacturers that they should play down their realistic toy weapon lines.
—An organized protest over the Nomad action figures, the "good" and "evil" Arab twins in the Rambo line created by Coleco Industries, brought about removal of the action figures from the market. Organized because of the negative stereotypes conveyed by the dolls, the protest represents the first successful effort we know in which a toy company voluntarily removed a war toy from the market because of the values it represented.

◆ **Groups have formed to work against the sale of war toys at the local level.**
—The Boston Area Task Force Against War Toys held a press conference at which it presented awards to area toy stores which did not sell war toys. Among the speakers was the Massachusetts Commissioner of Public Health who addressed the relationship between the sale of war toys and violence in society. The event was widely covered in the media.
—A group of citizens in Santa Cruz, California, have taken a multifaceted approach. They have been working with individual toy store merchants and have reached a voluntary ban on the sale of war toys at their stores. They have gotten other merchants to move their war toy displays away from prime locations in their stores. The group holds regular "Turn in War Toys" demonstrations and at the most recent one, received over 150 toys. Currently they are working with local officials to organize a "Turn-off TV" week in their town.
—A group of people in a city near Ottawa, Canada, bought up vast quantities of war toys with credit cards shortly before Christmas, so that toy stores had fewer to sell during the biggest toy-buying season. After Christmas, they returned the toys to the stores and got credit on their charge cards.
—A "Santa Claus" went to the war toy section of a major toy store and passed out a letter from Santa to children and adults which told them why these toys were harmful and should not be purchased.
—In Brooklyn, New York, members of Mobilization for Survival gathered at toy stores to sing Christmas carols with anti-war-toy lyrics. They distributed lyrics to the songs and invited shoppers to sing along with them.
—Members of Concerned Educators Allied for a Safe Environment, a national network of parents, teachers, and other advocates for young children sent out press releases calling for restoration of FCC television regulations to newspapers all over the United States before Christmas of 1988.
—The Los Angeles Alliance for Survival and the Dakin Toy Company joined together in 1988 with a toy trade-in. A child could send in a

toy gun or any other war-related toy (with two dollars to cover postage and handling) and receive a teddy bear in return.

—A group of war toy protesters gathered at a mock grave at the War Cannon Memorial in Santa Monica, California, to bury war toys. The toys were later dug up and sent to the War Toy Disarmament Project in Wells, Vermont, and transformed into a peace monument.

◆ **Parents and teachers have been working together to educate themselves on the issue of war play and war toys and to develop approaches that work for their situations.**

—A group of parents met in a daycare center in Brewster, Massachusetts to discuss war toys; they agreed to ban the giving of war toys as birthday presents among their children.

—Parents and teachers at many schools around the country have organized "TV turn-off" weeks. They have taken a variety of approaches to help children benefit from the experience including offering alternative activities to TV-watching at their schools during after-school hours, having children make their own games at school that they could play with their families during normal TV-viewing hours, and getting older children to keep journals about their reactions to withdrawal from television.

—A group of parents involved in the Parent Teachers Association in Massachusetts worked with the PTAs in neighboring towns to organize a lecture series on children and the media. It was so well received that followup lectures were planned for the following year.

Tangible efforts such as those described above can accomplish many things. They educate the public about the dangers of war toys and help set the stage for public dialogue about positive play environments for children. They send a message to manufacturers via the marketplace and alert them to public concern about their products. They pressure government to move toward more regulation and toward taking more responsibility for safeguarding the rights of children and families. And finally, they give parents and other concerned citizens effective avenues for working together and being heard; actions which provide participants with the sense of empowerment that they need to bring about meaningful change. A list of some of the many organizations that are working on issues relating to war toys and violence can be found in the final chapter of this book.

PART II

Practical Ideas and Resources for Dramatic Play

Providing interesting materials for dramatic play is a key to helping children get beyond the narrow and limiting war play which can result from too many single-purpose toys and violent TV cartoons. Here are some inexpensive alternative ideas and resources for war play which parents have told us about. They tap into the themes that often come up in war and superhero play but allow more room for children to develop their own ideas and take the play where they want it to go. They also help making rather than buying toys become a more important part of play.

Our suggestions for materials and how they might be used in dramatic play are not exhaustive. What transforms into an exciting "toy" and where it will lead your child is unpredictable. The only limits are your own and your child's imaginations!

9
Common Objects to Use as Toys and Props in War Play

Household Items

Since these items still have conventional uses in your home, you will probably need to establish some specific rules for each, for instance, when they can be used and where, and what to do with them when the play session is over.

Flashlight

Children love to play in darkened rooms. It makes things scarier and more dramatic. Playing with a flashlight can open up a world of possibilities for the kinds of dramatic effects which quickly capture young children's interest. It can help them work through fears of the dark that are so common in the early years.

Trips into dark outer space; hunts for ghosts and monsters that come out in the night; dangerous stormy sea voyages can all easily take place with such a prop. A flashlight might become a ray gun, walkie-talkie or transmitter of secret codes. The shadows created, elongated and enlarged—often mysterious and unpredictable—always do a lot to stimulate the kind of play themes that occur in war play.

Empty plastic laundry basket

If your child gets into a laundry basket, it can become a boat on the high seas, a canoe shooting the rapids or a tank. Get a slat of wood to use as an oar to paddle with or as a gun (if you allow this). If a storm occurs on the high seas, the boat may tip over and the passengers fall into the sea. Put a small pillow or baby blanket in and it's a bed (for He-Man while he's out on missions), a baby crib, a bird's nest. Turned upside down it becomes a cage for miniature dinosaurs or action figures —or even children—which keeps those outside it safe. When a child crawls around with it on her back, it's a turtle shell or an armored house.

Empty suitcases or briefcases

Pack it to take on journeys of all kinds: into outer space, to dinosaur land, on missions or to capture bad guys. Plan carefully what will be needed to take along (either pretend or real things) and there will be a variety of props to keep the action going as the scenario develops. This prop helps children plan ahead and develop their own ideas for what will happen in their play. It also taps into children's need to work out separation issues with parents—going away and coming back—where they can be in complete control.

Pillows

In addition to traditional pillow fights which can fit nicely into war play scenarios as a less violent way to carry out battles, pillows offer many other appealing possibilities for dramatic play. Make a pile of them on the floor and create a mountain for climbing over or for the dinosaurs or superman to knock down with their brute strength. Arrange them in a circle or boat shape and they provide protection or form a ship for a voyage. Or, put them in a straight line and they can be a barrier or wall between the good and bad guys' territory. Put dinosaurs or action figures underneath and they can sneak out and scare others too.

Lunchboxes or other small containers that latch shut

Pack real or pretend snacks in a lunchbox to take on adventures. Try to bring snacks that will replenish your energy after the hard work of the adventure. Doing "real" things as part of war play scenarios can help humanize the play.

Lunchboxes can also be used to make little portable adventure kits. Put in a magnifying glass, a notebook and pencil to help detectives search for clues. Put in handcuffs and a badge to be a police officer. Cotton balls, an empty medicine bottle and torn strips of old sheets make a doctor's bag or ambulance kit. Your child will come up with her own ideas about items to add.

Odds and ends of string and yarn

String, yarn and rope work well for making traps or webs to capture monsters, ghosts and bad guys. Toys can be tied up and held captive. Strings hung down from a closet pole or in a doorway are like cobwebs for crawling through. Make a "secret trail" with a length of string to help guide "Hansel and Gretel" (from the classic fairy tale) safely home. (Making a set of fifteen or twenty cardboard arrows—about eight by three inches—provides another way for children to make paths and routes for characters to follow.) A rope tied between two pieces of furniture can be a pretend tightrope and used for walking between "mountains." String is also great for tying props and costumes onto toys or children.

Warnings: Don't expect to use the yarn or string again unless you spend a lot of time helping to untangle and rewind it. The heavier its weight the easier this will be. If you get a long piece of rope, like a clothesline, it will become a regular feature in your child's dramatic play. *Before* you let a child have such a prop, make sure he clearly understands that it is not to go around his, or anyone else's, neck.

Common kitchen tools

Utensils like funnels, gravy basters, wooden spoons and plastic strainers are great for adding to all kinds of dramatic adventures. They are especially good for promoting play in the bathtub—one of the great settings for dramatic play that is often overlooked. During a bath, children are without their usual dramatic play toys and the open-endedness of the water with a few kitchen props can lead their play in many original directions. When you try this, plan to allow extra time for the bath in case your child wants it.

Household Objects You Usually Throw Away

Plastic liquid squirt and spray bottles

Save empty dishwashing liquid-type bottles or cleaning detergent spray bottles. Give these a good cleaning and fill them with water and they're great for play outside and in the bathtub. Children enjoy using them as play weapons (water pistols) which can do much more than the usual toy guns. Squirt water to give baths to both dolls and other small plastic figures. Mix a little shampoo in the bathtub and give the bottle a shake and you can squirt out bubbly water. Add a little color with a few drops of food coloring and it becomes a magic potion or "poison" to get monsters, cast spells or render the bad guys weak and helpless. The food coloring mixture is also great after snowfalls when children can paint on or write messages in the snow.

One parent described how her six-year-old son, who was not allowed toy guns, became a pacesetter in the neighborhood with his squirt bottle. The local gang began collecting their own squirt bottle weapons and trying out various soaps and colors for different effects.

Cardboard tubes

Save empty tubes from toilet paper, paper towels and food wraps. There are endless uses for these and a never-ending supply. Walkie-talkies (see Chapter Ten—"Things to Make") and megaphones, pretend weapons and hideouts for miniature figures are all common ways children put these to use. Decorate them with things like scraps of shiny or stickyback paper or dried beans and let your child's imagination take over.

Plastic mesh bags

Save the mesh bags onions and citrus fruit often come in. Children love using them as masks. They are great for creating a monster effect by distorting the hair and facial features.

Empty boxes all sizes

An assortment of empty food boxes can stimulate interesting dramatic play. Your child can pretend to cook a meal or pack a meal to take on adventures.

Boxes with lids, such as shoe boxes, can be used for packing and storing treasures. Larger lids, with a handle glued in the middle of one side, make great shields for knights. Young children like using boxes with lids as cages for captured things and for hiding secret treasures. With older children, shoe boxes are ideal for making little miniature worlds. Ezra Jack Keats' book, *The Trip*, provides a wonderful starting point for small world model making by showing children how to make a scene out of a shoe box like the one in which Louie traveled in the story.

Old blankets, sheets, large pieces of fabric and fabric remnants

These are very useful for all kinds of dramatic play. Draping an old blanket or sheet between a few chairs or over a table makes a great hideout. An old sheet torn into strips makes great bandages. Cut out a circle in the center of a rectangle of fabric to make a costume or use it for a cape.

Buttons

A button collection (once children are old enough not to put them in their mouths) can be used for pretend food or money. Shiny metal buttons make great pirate treasures. Or string some onto a piece of thin plastic-coated electrical wire to make a magical necklace.

Old adult clothes, hats, scarves and jewelry

An assortment of these can be used in endless combinations to make costumes for dramatic roles. It may be helpful to cut the sleeves of tops and legs of bottoms shorter so your child won't get tangled up in them. They can be decorated with stickers or felt-tip pens. Children often assign magical powers to jewelry, for instance, a ring with a special stone that can cast a spell or give invisible protection to its wearer.

Inexpensive Things to Collect Outside the Home

Items to ask for at stores

Hardware stores

Here you will find many possibilities for materials depending on the store and your timing. If they cut new keys, they may have a collection of old, unwanted keys they are willing to give you. If they sell locks, they may also have some old locks with keys. Keys and locks are great for all kinds of mysteries and adventures. Figuring out what key fits in which lock, carrying around a ring of interesting keys, having a magic key which can fit all doors are ways children can use these props in their mysteries and adventures. You might also try using a key in story-telling, for instance, "What will we find behind the door that this key opens?" Children also enjoy sorting and matching keys.

Hardware stores often have old wallpaper sample books (new editions come out annually so find out when the old ones will be replaced). The wallpaper can be glued onto large cartons being made into play houses and vehicles. (See "Constructions from cardboard cartons" in Chapter Ten—"Things to Make".) Older children can glue wallpaper into smaller boxes (like shoe boxes) to create miniature houses and fantasy worlds. Wallpaper samples are also useful for all kinds of story writing and art projects—the paper is strong and cheap.

You can also ask about old linoleum and ceramic tile samples at hardware and flooring stores. These can be used again and again with blocks or permanently laid in box buildings to tile roofs or floors, or to make secret paths or stepping stones to follow along (like the yellow brick road in *The Wizard of Oz*). This type of play may even help your child with counting and measuring skills.

Supermarkets

Supermarkets and produce stores offer interesting scrounge possibilities. See what your child finds to do with these items: colorful, sectioned cardboard trays from the produce section which are discarded once they are empty; styrofoam meat packing trays; plastic cherry tomato webbed trays (great as miniature cages); empty egg cartons; corrugated boxes in which food products are shipped.

Seafood markets and restaurants

Take a bag and ask for a collection of clam, oyster and scallop shells.

Fabric and carpet stores

You can often get free or inexpensive pieces of fabric remnants (try to get interesting colors and textures) from fabric stores to use for costumes, scenery and easily disassembled "buildings." You can also do interesting things with the long cardboard tubes on which fabric often comes (see Chapter Ten—"Things to Make").

Carpet scraps or sample squares are great for flooring "buildings," either temporarily or permanently. We know a girl who endlessly used a special carpet square as a "magic carpet" for taking fantasy voyages. Reading your child the story of the magic carpet is a good way to help this theme along.

Lumber yards and building sites

Go with a box to collect wood scraps. Softer woods, like some pines, are easier for hammering through; check for splinters and have sandpaper handy. Younger children can make their own toys and props by coloring individual pieces of wood with felt-tip pens or by gluing pieces of wood together, although waiting for them to dry can be hard. They also often enjoy sanding their toys. Older children can accomplish a lot with a hammer and nails—a safety lesson and a little help and adult supervision will be needed initially. If you know a carpenter or see one working, she may also be willing to save you scraps.

At a building site you might also find other interesting discarded materials, for instance, unneeded pieces of pipe or plastic-coated electrical or telephone wire.

Optical stores

Here you will often be able to get old eyeglass frames, with glass lenses taken out. These are perfect for disguises and costumes. You can also ask for discarded plastic lenses which children enjoy using as magnifying glasses and to create special effects.

Collecting at yard sales and on scouting trips around the neighborhood

Children find it very appealing to have "real things," things they have seen used by adults, to use as props in their play. Such items can help them feel more grown-up and can add an increased element of realism and seriousness to their play.

The kinds of things we list here might be found on your street on garbage collection day or, they might be found at yard sales. If you remain vigilant and have a bit of good luck, you might be able to acquire some of the following treasures for your children in their play.

Telephones

Telephones encourage all kinds of dramatic play. Children can have conversations with each other and be like the adults they have seen using phones for calling the doctor, talking to relatives or doing office work. Children also enjoy taking telephones apart. And this can help take some of the magical quality out of the telephone as children see what is really inside it!

A steering wheel

Putting a steering wheel into a pretend vehicle adds an exciting dimension to imaginary journeys and adventures or to the reenactment of outings they have had with families.

An oar or paddle

This can help make sea voyages more exciting and real. Your child will probably come up with other original uses too.

Doorknobs

Who knows what your child will do with these; perhaps they'll be used for opening imaginary and mysterious doors.

A typewriter

This is usually popular whether any of the keys work or not. Put in a piece of paper and children can write secret messages or messages in code. They will often pretend it is a transmitter for sending messages. A typewriter also often leads to office play.

Old clocks

This can become a time machine, moving the child forward and backward in time at the turn of a dial.

Large appliance cartons

You can often find a large carton out on the street on garbage collection day. This is a great treasure. Children love to climb in and out of large boxes. If there is a cover they often enjoy closing it and sitting in the dark, which can lead to scary imaginary adventures especially with a flashlight. For younger children, peek-a-boo might be a favorite use. There are also an endless variety of things you can make the boxes into. (See Chapter Ten—"Things to Make".)

Tires

Often available in the trash or given away by service stations, old tires are very useful in outdoor adventures. They are fun to climb on or get into as boats or to make into a heap for climbing on. Put a plank or planks between two or more tires to make a bridge over a jungle river or a gangplank on a pirate's ship, as in *Peter Pan*.

A section of an old tree trunk

A tree trunk can be used with tires to help set the stage for an adventure. Children also seem to enjoy pounding nails into it and also trying to hollow the inside out as a secret hiding place for toys. It can also make a good table to use when having real or pretend snacks while out on missions.

A camping tent

A tent provides the perfect hideout, headquarters or clubhouse. It will be the focal point for endless hours of play. Children will love setting up the environment inside with old blankets, food supplies, adventure equipment such as flashlights and rope. Other old camping equipment will also be well used. Don't be surprised by the child who wants to move into it for a few days!

10
Things to Make

Recipes

The following recipes for open-ended play materials and mixtures can be made from common household ingredients. In addition to offering children the opportunity to mess, experiment and create, they also lend themselves very naturally to fantasy play. Often, as children are pounding, rolling and molding, little dramatic scenes develop with accompanying monologue and sound effects. Usually, with younger children and sometimes with older ones, the process of transforming and interacting with the material will be more important than having a product to save at the end. Some of these recipes cannot even lead to a final product but help children get involved in the process of messing. With others, it is possible to make and save something which could even be used as a prop for play later on.

These recipes can save the day when you want to divert children away from war play (maybe it's gotten out of hand or you've just had enough) or on rainy days when TV seems like the only way for everyone to keep their sanity. Try making one of these recipes with your child. She can learn a lot from the experience and will be more invested in using the finished product. With young children, you will probably want to measure, and they can pour the ingredients in and mix. With older children, you can involve them fully in the process. Try making a simple recipe with pictures that even nonreaders can learn to follow. Once a recipe has been made a few times, older children can begin making it on their own.

Basic playdough

Ingredients:
2 cups flour
1 cup salt
2 tablespoons vegetable oil
5-6 drops food coloring or 1 tablespoon tempera paint
1 cup water (approximate)

Cooked Play Dough

3 cups flour

1½ cups salt

2 table spoons cream of tartar

3 tablespoons oil

3 cups water

1. Put everything in a big pot

2. Cook and stir

3. When just warm knead

4. Play

Recipes with simple drawings can help children participate in cooking activities.

Put flour, salt and oil in bowl. Mix water and coloring. Gradually add colored water and stir. When ingredients begin to stick together, knead with hands. Add more water bit by bit until malleable but not sticky. Store it in a sealed plastic container or plastic bag in the refrigerator and it should last for several weeks.

Items your child makes can be left out to dry. They should not be more than about two inches thick in any one place or the inside can't dry and the outside cracks as it dries. Once fully dried and hardened, they can be painted with tempera paint. Brown playdough, which can be made from mixing all the food colors together, seems to be especially appealing for the dramatic play with younger children (which may have to do with their deep interest in toilet training!). You can add various scents to the playdough, such as vanilla, almond or lemon extract, if you think your child can refrain from eating the dough.

Cooked playdough (see illustration facing page)

Ingredients:
3 cups flour
1 cup salt
3 cups water
2 tablespoons cream of tartar (in the spice department of grocery stores)
3 tablespoons vegetable oil
a few drops food coloring or 1 tablespoon tempera paint

Mix ingredients in a large pot. Place over a low heat and stir constantly until mixture begins to thicken to a consistency like mashed potatoes. Remove from heat. Scrape into a bowl or pan. When it cools enough to safely touch, knead vigorously with hands. This keeps a very long time in a sealed container in the refrigerator and also dries nicely if the objects aren't too thick.

Oobleck

Ingredients:
1 cup cornstarch
a few drops food coloring
water

Put the cornstarch in a bowl. Slowly mix in the water, mixing constantly with your hand. When most of the powder is gone it should be about ready, but you will have to decide when it gets to a consistency you like. This mixture is indescribable until you try it yourself. It should be runny but stick together. Add drops of food color once you begin playing with it. Oobleck dries out quickly; just add a bit more water to get it going again.

Named after the substance in Dr. Seuss's book, *Bartholomew and the Oobleck,* this mixture provides great fun for children and adults alike. Try pouring your Oobleck into a roasting pan or cookie sheet so it can spread out. Try holding it in your hand and see what happens. Try pushing your fist into it. How long can you keep it rolled up in a ball? Can you make up a story about it?

Helpful hint: When you get a big mess, which often happens with Oobleck, don't panic. It has the amazing ability to brush off clothes, or be swept or vacuumed up as soon as it dries.

Silly Slime

Ingredients:
1 cup Elmer's Glue
about 1 cup liquid laundry starch (in the cleaning products section of supermarkets)
a few drops food color or tempera paint

Pour Elmer's Glue into a bowl. Mix in the color with the glue (colored glue is also a nice addition to regular gluing projects). Gradually stir in the laundry starch. Use a metal spoon because it can stick to porous wooden spoons. As the mixture starts to become stringy, add just a little more starch. Knead vigorously with your hands. If it continues sticking to your hands, add a little more starch. When it stops sticking to you it is ready for use. This saves very well in a sealed container in the refrigerator.

Try stretching it out into strings; hanging it over a table and letting it drip down; holding it while someone else stretches it across a room; hiding small plastic toys in it. Because of its physical properties, it can foster dramatic scenarios about making traps to catch bad guys or being "The Blob."

Helpful hint: This sticks to anything that can absorb water like paper, pourous wood, or clothing and gets hard like rock when it dries. We suggest using this mixture in the kitchen. But if it does get absorbed into something it shouldn't, very hot water will soften it and wash it out.

Warning: This mixture is not to be used with any child who might put it in her mouth because laundry starch can be toxic if eaten. Have children wash their hands after they use it.

Edible pretzel playdough

Ingredients:
1 package yeast (in refrigerator section of grocery stores)
4 cups flour
1 1/2 cups warm water
1 tablespoon sugar
1 teaspoon salt
1 egg

In a bowl, mix the yeast, warm water, sugar and salt. You can add a few drops of food coloring if desired. Gradually mix in flour. Save the egg. When the dough begins holding together, pour it out onto a table and knead vigorously until it's smooth and the consistency of playdough. Play with it as playdough and when you're ready, make it into shapes and objects about the size of large pretzels. Place them onto a cookie sheet that is covered with aluminum foil. Using a very clean paint brush or basting brush, brush the pretzels with beaten egg. Bake at 425° for 12–15 minutes or until golden brown.

Children can eat the monsters they make—the ultimate sense of power and control!

Sawdust playdough

Ingredients:
2 cups fine sawdust
1 cup flour
1 tablespoon glue
hot water or liquid starch
food coloring or tempera paint

Combine sawdust, flour and glue in a bowl. Slowly add the water or starch which has the coloring added. Stop when the mixture reaches the consistency of playdough.

Sawdust playdough is an inexpensive way to make a lot of dough. You can usually get sawdust at a lumber yard under its saws. Just go there with a bag and ask. This mixture dries nicely. If you're making something thick, hollow out the inside and turn it over after a day so the bottom dries. When it dries it can be smoothed with sand paper and painted.

This mixture is wonderful for children who have become interested in making models and miniature scenes. It can be used to make buildings, castle walls, or puppet heads (hollow them out so a finger can fit inside).

Warning: Be sure the sawdust you use for this recipe comes from *pure wood,* not particle board or pressed board. They have other things in them besides wood that can be harmful if inhaled. Also, be careful for sawdust that has splinters; use fine-textured sawdust.

Recipe ingredients to keep on hand

> flour
> salt
> liquid laundry starch
> cornstarch
> vegetable oil
> cream of tartar
> Elmers Glue
> food coloring and/or tempera paint

Useful props to use with these mixtures

These simple things often lead to more creative play than commercially made playdough toy sets.

> garlic press—squeeze playdough through to make thin spagetti-like strands
> rolling pin
> nonserrated, dull knife
> craft sticks (popsicle sticks)
> toothpicks (with older children)
> forks
> metal or wood meat mallet
> small metal or plastic containers
> collection of miniature farm or zoo animals or dinosaurs

It's usually good to start with few or no props so your child will explore the material and what it can do first. But sometimes, bringing out a simple prop can help children get involved if they're having trouble getting started. When you introduce props, just offer one or two things at a time so your child can explore the possibilities they offer before moving onto the next thing. Eventually you may want to get a container to keep special props in, to which your child can have easy access.

Hint: Props such as those suggested above can often stimulate more creative and imaginative play than those sold at stores specifically as "playdough or clay toys." We recommend staying away from cookie cutters, the most commonly used playdough toys, until children have had a lot of experience using the dough, because they tend to limit what children do.

Toys, Props and Costumes to Make at Home

Walkie-talkies

Walkie-talkies offer children endless opportunities for adding to their dramatic play. They provide an alternative to guns and weapons as props for war play, they suggest doing actions other than fighting and they foster communication and cooperation among players—all reasons for encouraging their use. And, children seem to find the idea of verbalizing commands and messages to each other extremely appealing.

Children are amazingly versatile at using a wide variety of things to represent walkie-talkies in their play. Those commonly used range from the expensive, battery-operated ones that are attached to helmets or belts and really transmit radio signals across large distances, to those which merely suggest the idea of pretending to send a message. All types offer certain special opportunities for enriching dramatic play, but we do not feel the fancy radio transmitting ones are worth the price, especially until the simpler varieties have been developed fully in play.

Nonfunctioning walkie-talkies

Small wooden blocks with things hammered in or glued on

All you need is a small block of scrap wood, sanded to protect against splinters, a few nails and a hammer. Children love to add their own little features. Rarely will it just be for talking into; usually it will take on many magical powers that the child invents. "Press this button (a nail or sticker glued on) and you can get bigger"; "this button makes you invisible"; and, "that one makes your voice really loud."

Cardboard tubes (from toilet paper) wrapped in aluminum foil

This simple, always available variety of walkie-talkie is great when several children want to play. You can make enough to go around and everyone can join in the fun with no disputes over sharing.

Funnels

This type of walkie-talkie is often very popular. It looks right and is easy to hold on to. When you talk into the big end, you can give a secret message to your partner who puts her ear near the thin end.

Funny things happen with voices when you do this. And you can make bigger, magnified noises when you talk through the small end.

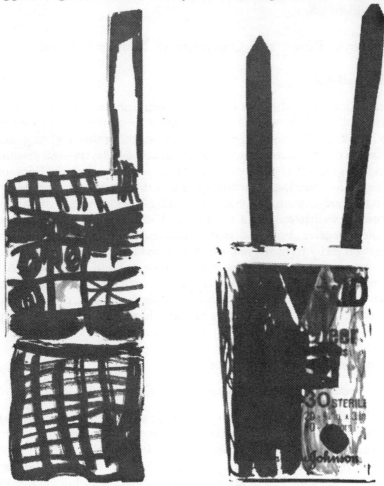

Band-aid boxes or cardboard are all that's needed to make a homemade walkie-talkie.

Walkie-talkies that really work

Clear plastic, flexible tubing

Tubing 1/4- to 1/2-inch in diameter and 1 to 5 yards long is available in assorted widths by the foot or yard at hardware stores.

Plastic tubing walkie-talkies actually do carry and magnify sound that others can hear across the full distance of the tube (so the longer the tube is, the more exciting the effect). Because it's flexible, it can go around corners so you can send and receive messages when you can't see the other person. Children love the "magic" created by this simple prop. At first, younger children will have a hard time learning to put the tube to their ears to receive messages, especially when they can't see the person sending the messages; so with them, you may want to begin with a shorter tube and an adult as the message sender.

Additional uses: Cut into one- or two-foot pieces, this tubing is a great bath toy (once your child has learned to blow out and not suck in). It can also be a wonderful bubble blower—just put one end into a large container with diluted dishwashing detergent.

Long heavy cardboard tubes

Large bolts of fabric come wound onto these tubes. You can get these free once they are empty. Fabric stores often save them, but if not, they might save some for you if you agree to come for them at a specified time.

Try whispering through one end of the tube into your child's ear. A surprising thing happens. Once the excitement of this walkie-talkie wears off, use 2-inch masking tape to attach two or more tubes together, end-to-end. Tape the ends so that there is about a half inch space between the tubes underneath the tape. This will allow the tubes to bend around corners at the joints so messages can be sent between rooms.

Additional uses: These tubes, used either singly or taped together, make great marble runs. Just prop up the tube a few inches and send marbles through. Try varying the height to see how to make a marble go the fastest, the furthest. You can also use them for peek-a-boo games with young children. For instance, have your child watch you put several small objects in one end and try to guess what will come out first, second, third, etc. when you tip the tube. Try tipping it so sometimes the first item put in comes out first and sometimes the last item comes out first. The tubes are also great for making child-size structures that children can crawl inside of. (See the next section.)

Buildings and enclosures

A simple enclosure can provide the focal point for play scenarios. Children usually love to have things they can fit inside to use as part of the stage sets for their play. Their usual environment is scaled to adults' size, so they like having little spaces which are just the right size for them. An enclosure also creates a place where they can shut out the adult world and just pretend. Whether it's "He-Man's castle" or a space ship, enclosures provide children with an open-ended prop which can change and evolve with their play. Here are a few you might want to try.

Constructions from cardboard cartons

Hint: None of these items will last forever, but when one goes, it's an opportunity to try making another! A large serrated knife or mat knife works well cutting all but the heaviest corrugated cardboard.

A house

Find a carton big enough for one or more children to fit into—large appliance cartons are especially good. Tape the openings shut. Mark places for a door and windows on the walls. Remember to only cut out three sides of the door so it can open and close. You may want to do the same for the windows so they can be open and shut. Or, make a circular door just big enough for your child to crawl through which can be a "rabbit hole." What the building gets named will most likely depend on the themes children are currently using in their play. Initially, children will probably want to play with it just like this, but after a while there are a lot of additional things you can do. Decide with your child how to decorate it:

> —The inside and outside walls can be painted with tempera paint. Try using inexpensive real painter's brushes for this (larger than the kind used for art projects). We recommend doing this task outside if possible, or on a kitchen floor well protected with newspapers. When it comes to painting the inside, your child may need some help figuring out how to keep from leaning on a wet wall while painting another. But do expect some of the paint to end up in places other than the walls.
> —Put carpet remnants or linoleum tile samples on the floor.
> —Wallpaper the walls with sheets of paper from wallpaper sample books. A mixture of flour and water, or diluted Elmer's Glue spread with large painter's brushes works well.
> —Make curtains for the windows. Taping fabric scraps onto the inside of the windows works well.
> —Attach a few self-sticking hooks onto the inside walls for hanging costumes and props on.
> —Make a few paintings or drawings for the walls.

A space ship

Seal up the ends of the carton. Make a circular "hatch" opening your child can fit through. Options for decorating the ship are listed on the following page.

—Cover the outside and/or the inside with aluminum foil or metallic wallpaper using tape or diluted glue so it looks like metal.
—Draw a control panel on the inside; or you can make one. Attach old hardware—such as chains, various locks and clasps, and gears—to a board, or stick small objects onto one wall by gluing them on (for instance, small pieces of dowel, wooden spools, buttons or clips). Put on a small bicycle bell. This control panel is well worth the effort; it can be used for all kinds of other vehicles and adventures.

An example of a "space ship control panel" made from old locks and chains.

—For piloting the ship put in an old steering wheel or stick one end of a 12-inch wooden dowel through a wall and put a circular piece of heavy cardboard onto the other end so it can be used for steering.
—Connect a walkie-talkie (see earlier section). You can establish communication with the outside world by making a hole in a wall and pushing the clear plastic tubing walkie-talkie through.

A castle

Put the large side of a carton on the floor and cut off the top (the other large side). Then cut square pieces out of the top of all the walls to create "lookout stations." Cut out a door removing the cardboard completely.

Use the piece of cardboard taken out for the door to make a "portcullis" (gate that lifts up and down) or drawbridge. Cut squares out of the door to create a grid effect. Attach a rope to a hole at the top of the gate. Put the gate outside the castle in front of the door opening and put the rope over the top of the castle wall. Pulling on the rope opens the portcullis.

Paint the castle to look like stonework.

A castle made out of a large cardboard box can contribute to hours of creative play.

Cars, trucks and buses

Rectangular cartons work best for these. They don't have to be as big as for the houses. Cut out the bottom of the carton (large retangular side). Cut a square or rectangular hole in the center or the large side on the top of the box. It should be big enough for a child to fit through (don't cut all the way to the side walls). The walls should be about 2-feet high so that when a child kneels down inside, his head and shoulders come down through the hole on top. Cut the walls shorter along the bottom as needed.

You can make the vehicle "go" by kneeling down on the floor with your head coming through the top hole and crawling around on your knees. Make the hole on top bigger and a passenger can crawl around with the driver.

Paint it the color of the vehicle you want—for instance, black for a police car, yellow for a school bus.

Attach a circular piece of cardboard to one end of a wooden dowel and stick the other end into the front top of the vehicle, and you have a steering wheel.

Glue, draw or paint large circles onto the front walls for headlights. Do the same on the sides for wheels.

Attach cardboard wings on the side to make an airplane.

With smaller boxes, use the same basic design but attach cloth or rope straps from front to back on both sides of the opening. Children can wear the straps on their shoulders and carry them around to make them go.

Constructions from heavy cardboard tubes

The 4- to 5-foot cardboard tubes available from fabric stores can make a wonderful building. You can fasten six tubes together to make a three-dimensional triangular teepee-like frame. Poke a hole about one inch from the ends of the tubes to be used for attaching the tubes together. Use heavy string or plastic-coated wire to join the ends together as shown in the diagram below. Don't make the string too tight so the tubes can just bend at the joints. See the illustration below to see how to join all the ends. Cover the frame with a large sheet or blanket and you have a cozy playhouse, camping tent or rocket ship. Two children will be able to fit inside comfortably.

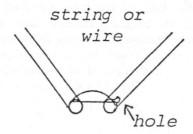

string or wire

hole

Method for attaching cardboard tubes

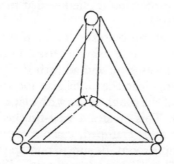

Finished cardboard tube frame (tetrahedron)

Costumes

Costumes can do a lot to help children take on dramatic roles in their play. Most of what we provide doesn't have to be very realistic or detailed. Often just having an assortment of old adult clothing, pieces of cloth and old scarves available is all children need to design their own original costumes. But when you want to provide a costume for a specific role, capturing the most pronounced and concrete aspects of a character's costume is usually all that is needed. This can allow room for children to add their own additions and modifications to the costume as well as to have the definition of what the costume represents change and evolve with the play.

Fantasy capes

Many superheroes wear capes, and you can make one easily with a piece of velvet, of colorful shiny fabric like the kind used as lining for clothes, or even a towel. Cut it into a rectangle with the long side a bit shorter than your child. If you have a sewing machine, make a small hem around all the edges. If not, put iron-on bias tape (found at stores in the sewing section) or colored masking tape (available at hardware stores) around the edges. Put a fastener at the neck. A small strip of velcro works well. You can often find self-adhesive velcro, but for durability you may need to add a few stitches. A large diaper pin can also do the job.

Helmets

Children usually love head coverings of all kinds. There is something about putting on a helmet—maybe because of the adult roles it conjures up or the feeling of protection it offers—that makes it one of the most popular head coverings.

One of our favorites can be made from a plastic gallon milk carton. Cut off the spout and handle using a serrated knife (do this yourself). With a bit of head measuring and adjusting of what is cut away, you can create an opening just the right size for your child's head to fit in. Tape around all of the rough edges with black electric tape (available at hardware stores). This creates a well-finished and official look. If your child's head is a bit cramped, cut out the circle indentations on the bottle to make more room. Be sure to put tape around these too.

You can tape a piece of heavy clear plastic—like the kind that comes on "see through" toy boxes so you can see the toy inside—onto the front to make a visor. Or, you can attach it with brass paper fasteners so that it can slide up and down. *Warning:* Make sure the plastic is heavy enough so that it cannot stick to your child's face and cause suffocation.

Children can use this helmet for many different roles—for instance, as part of an astronaut's, knight's or superhero's costume, or as a motorcycle, police officer or speed racer helmet.

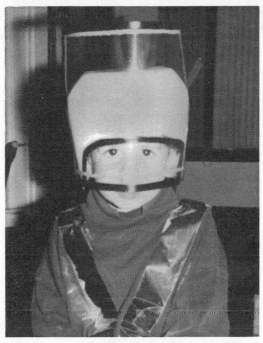

An example of a space helmet made from a gallon milk carton, electrical tape and clear plastic film.

Knight's Costume

To make a tabbard (knight's robe) take a shiny piece of rectangular fabric, like that used to line clothing, about 4 feet long and 1 foot wide. Hem or tape the edges. Cut a 6-inch square or circle in the center (hem or tape). Draw a design on the front with a permanent felt-tip pen or make a design with black electrical tape. Hold it in place with a belt which can also serve as a sword holder.

You can make armor with thick cardboard. Cut out two pieces for each arm—one above and one below the elbow. Do the same for the legs. The pieces should only go on the fronts of the arms and legs. Cut out a chest piece. Paint the front of the pieces silver or use a silver felt-tip pen or crayon. Gluing on aluminum foil also works, but is less durable. Use a 1/2- to 1-inch-wide elastic (available from sewing sections of stores) to join together the arm pieces and leg pieces. Brass

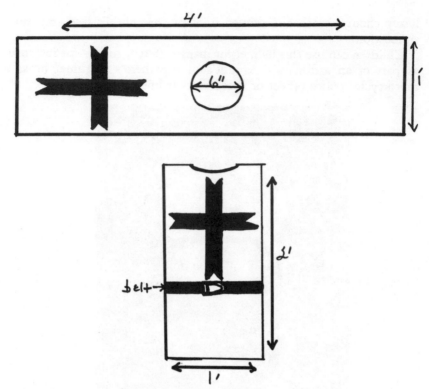

Here is the illustration to use for making a tabbard.

paper fasteners work well for this. Also use this elastic to make loops on the armor that go around your child's arms, legs and chest.

Warning: This takes work to get on and is probably too complicated for younger children, but four or five year olds who are very involved in knight play love it.

You can make a shield with a piece of heavy cardboard about 18 by 18 inches big. Make it pointed at the bottom. Paint or color it silver. When this is dry paint or draw on a simple coat of arms. Use brass paper fasteners to attach two strips of heavy elastic in the center of the back (parallel to each other and vertical to the floor when the shield is held) which your child can put his arm through.

A sword can be made by first gluing and then hammering together two strips of well-sanded wood, one about 2 feet long the other about 6 to 8 inches. Put the short piece about 6 inches down one end of the long piece. It is advisable not to make the end pointed, but children can sand the end to round the corners.

A child dressed up in cardboard armor with homemade sword and shield.

Astronaut's costume

Get an old dark-colored adult turtleneck shirt. Cut off the sleeves to the length of your child's arms. Cut heavy aluminum foil into strips and glue them on the shirt to look like metal. This also works well for a knight's costume.

To make oxygen tanks, take two empty, large plastic soda bottles. Attach them together at the top and bottom (so they are parallel and about 4 inches apart). Tie a heavy piece of string or ribbon to the top of each bottle. You can put the bottles on your child's back and tie them on around her chest or each shoulder. Tape one end of a 12-inch piece of clear plastic tubing to the inside of one bottle. The child can put the other piece into her mouth to pretend to be breathing the air. These also are popular for sea diver costumes.

An astronaut ready for take-off in homemade costume with "oxygen tanks."

Animal costumes

There are many simple, wild (and other) animal costumes you can make. Here are a few suggestions for how to begin. Take a dark, solid-colored turtleneck shirt and firmly attach a tail to the bottom of the back. Good tails can be made by sewing a strip of simulated fur—available at fabric stores—into a thin tube, or by stuffing an old knee-sock with old stockings or rags. You can tape or glue cardboard ears onto a child's stiff plastic headband. Used together, the tail and ears can suggest many different animals—from mice and rats, to cats and jaguars. There are other things you can add to make this costume more like a child's favorite animals or animal characters. For instance, attaching a large red bow to the front of the shirt makes the mischievous "Cat in the Hat," the popular character from Dr. Seuss' books.

You can make a leopard by gluing large black spots onto an old pair of tights and solid-colored polo or turtleneck shirt. Taping on horizontal stripes or drawing them with a permanent ink black marker can make a zebra or tiger.

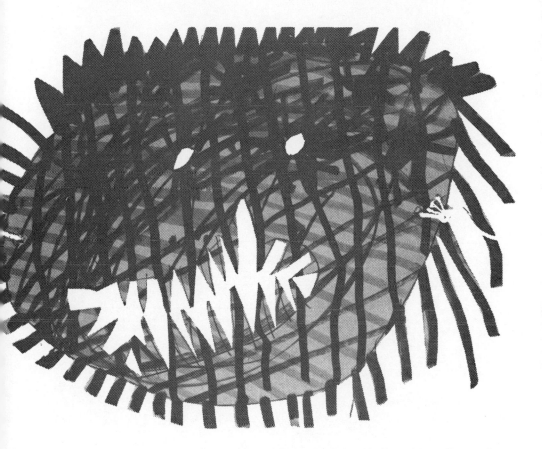

One child started an animal costume by making a lion mask.

11

"Wild Things" Not "War Things"

Using Children's Books to Foster Dramatic Play

There are many children's books which appeal to the same interests and needs in children that are targeted by violent television programs and their accompanying toys. But you have probably noticed that television cartoons provide children with very powerful stimuli for dramatic play and it can be hard to compete with their content by reading an occasional book.

There are several things you can do to increase the influence books have on your child's play:

◆ **Set up a routine for choosing new books to read.**

You might, for example go to the public library regularly. Pick out books together. Browsing can be fun. But also discuss the kinds of books you both would like to look for before you go and while you are there.

◆ **Select books that relate to themes present in your child's dramatic play.**

If your child has been using boats a lot you might plan to look for books about fictional adventures on the high seas as well as nonfiction books about boats and real sea voyages.

◆ **Try to choose books that have dramatic events, powerful characters, appealing illustrations, and special features that can be easily dramatized or add a new dimension to your child's play.**

For example, in Dr. Seuss's *Bartholomew and the Oobleck,* the idea of a gooey substance falling from the sky and wreaking havoc on the kingdom will grab many children. (See "Recipes" section of Chapter Ten—"Things to Make.") The magical powers of Moony's scary drawings to come alive in David McPhail's *The Magical Drawings of*

Moony B. Finch, offer a powerful springboard for play. A book like *The Three Billy Goats Gruff* lends itself to a dramatization of the entire story with a bridge, a troll and billy goats with small, medium and large voices. John Burningham's book, *Come Away From the Water, Shirley,* in which Shirley has an imaginary sea voyage, meets pirates and finds a treasure map that leads her to buried treasure, can suggest hunting for treasure and making treasure maps. And the Dr. Seuss creation, *The Cat in the Hat,* provides children with a wonderfully mischievous and clever character to bring into their play.

◆ **Read favorite books over and over and return to them at regular intervals rather than always having a continuous stream of only new books.**

The stories which become the most meaningful and important to children are also the ones most likely to become a part of dramatic play. Often, on the first reading of a book, children just want to hear the story and find out the ending. With repeated readings children can begin to feel more personally comfortable and involved with the characters and plot. They begin to know what's on each page and to understand the story more deeply. This familiarity enables children to feel more confident reenacting the story in play.

◆ **Read books that have sequels or that have the same character(s) appearing again.**

One reason children enjoy TV series is that they get to know the characters as they see them again and again. Finding books that are part of a series can help children identify with a particular character and want to incorporate him or her into play. While some series books seem to have been written merely to capitalize on the success of an initial book or character and are not of the highest quality literature, there are also some fine books in this category. And if your child seems to be especially attracted to a character who is in a book without a sequel, try to make up your own sequel together.

One of our favorite series book characters for fostering dramatic play is Louie, created by Ezra Jack Keats. In the first book, *Louie,* Louie is mesmerized by a puppet show given by his friends; instructions for making a puppet from the story are provided at the end of the book. In *The Trip,* as Louie is making a "peep show" of a city skyscape in a shoe box, he looks in and takes an imaginary voyage back to his old neighborhood on Halloween; instructions are given for making a "peep show" like Louie's using a shoe box. And, in *Regards to the Man in the Moon,* Louie and his friends go on a space voyage in an old bathtub which only flies when they use their "imaginations." After reading this book, no child's bath play will ever be quite the same! In addition to creating a very sympathetic child who has a wonderful imagination, the *Louie* books incorporate much about cultural diversity and positive social relationships.

◆ **Choose a favorite author to get to know better.**

We often don't think to point out to children that people write books. And many young children do not stop to wonder where a story came from. But pointing out to children that people write stories from their own imaginations helps them realize that they too can become authors. In addition, by reading many books written by the same author to children, they begin to get to know that author—what to expect, how things are said, who the author cares about. All of this deepens a child's experience with books and the stories contained within their pages and increases the likelihood that content from the books will be brought into play.

There are a wide range of authors who have written many books which are particularly well-suited to fostering dramatic play. In addition to Ezra Jack Keats (mentioned above), you might try looking for the books of Eloise Greenfield (whose books reflect many aspects of Black American culture—for instance, *Me and Neesie*), Verna Aardema (who has retold some wonderful African folktales), Dr. Seuss, Steven Kellogg, Patricia McKissack (who writes about folktales she heard growing up in the South), Maurice Sendak, and Beatrix Potter (*Peter Rabbit* and other animal tales). When your child forms a special attachment with a particular book, try to find other books by the same author.

◆ **Try books which can get children interested in making up their own endings to the story.**

This can help them get more actively involved with a story as well as help them develop their own skill at story writing. For instance, in Steven Kellogg's, *The Mysterious Tadpole*, Louis receives a tadpole as a gift from his uncle which grows into an enormous friendly monster. Just as he solves the monster problem his uncle sends him an enormous egg that is about to hatch. It's anyone's guess what the egg will turn into!

◆ **Try to help children bring characters, dramatic events and salient aspects of books into their play by:**

    —making a suggestion based on a book when the time is ripe;
    —providing or making simple props, scenery or costumes to help dramatize the story.

◆ **Remember that it's important to use books that represent both boys and girls and children of a variety of backgrounds, races** and cultures. It's also crucial to try to find books that are as free from gender, racial, economic and ethnic stereotypes as possible.

Although the number of books that represent a more diverse world with fewer stereotypes is growing, it still takes extra effort to find them. Classic European fairy tales, beloved by many children and valuable in many ways, provide little in the way of cultural diversity and are full of gender stereotypes. If you look in a bookstore with children's books, the chances are you will still find at least two books about boys for every one about girls and the vast majority of books will represent the values and images of a white middle-class culture. It you decide to read a book to your child that does portray some race, class or sex biases, point these out and talk them over.

Providing children with books that portray the rich diversity of human experience will help to broaden their perspective of the world. It will help to counteract the very limited views about race, ethnicity, gender and class portrayed by TV and through toys. As children are exposed to a diverse range of characters and stories through books, they are likely to find vivid and meaningful content for their dramatic play.

If you have a hard time finding nonstereotyped, culturally diverse books in bookstores or the library, you can order inexpensive paperbacks by mail. (For instance, see Savanna Books in the "Resources" section of the following chapter.)

Ideas for Fostering Dramatic Play with Selected Books

Here are a few examples of how you might begin to help children weave elements of a book into their dramatic play. Don't expect your child to act out the story exactly as it was read. Young children won't bring the entire plot or correct sequence of a book into play; rather, they will pull out the pieces that are most dramatic and appealing to them and which resonate with their needs. As they do this, at first they are likely to imitate a character or action. But with time, they often begin to vary and add to the story elements. The play gets longer and the story often changes. As children get older, more of the details and logic of the story enter in. By about the age of six, some children begin to want to do realistic reenactments of the stories, often as plays.

As we've said before, there is no one suggestion or approach for using a book that will work with every child. But if you offer a variety of stories to choose from, your child will pick what is most meaningful at any given time. And, of course, even great suggestions won't always strike a responsive chord.

Who's in Rabbit's House? by Verna Aardema

This Masai tale provides a wonderful variation on the *Three Little Pigs* story. An unknown creature, "The Long One," moves into Rabbit's house and threatens to trample anyone who tries to enter. All of Rabbit's big animal friends offer to help get The Long One out using some violent method that will require destroying the house in the process. Finally, the little frog uses scary words instead of destruction to trick The Long One (who turns out to be only a caterpillar) into coming out. Wonderfully illustrated as a play with people wearing gorgeous animal masks, the animals are both males and females. The repetitiveness of the language and events, as animal after animal attempts to evict The Long One, helps draw young children into the excitement and humor of the story. The underlying messages that brain works better than brawn and that friends can help each other are both appealing alternatives to themes of aggression and competition seen on TV.

Many children will be able to make deep personal connections with the story. The idea that a scary thing might be less scary if we know more about it can help children with their own fears. The notion that even a little animal can outsmart an unknown bully can fortify a child's feelings of confidence. And seeing that clever words can solve this problem provides children with an effective model for resolving conflict nonviolently.

There are a variety of features in this book that lend themselves to dramatic play. Any enclosure big enough for a child to fit in, like a large cardboard carton with a door cut in it or a table with a cloth draped over it to make sides, can easily become Rabbit's house. Children enjoy playing the roles of the animals outside the house, as well as The Long One. They can bring in any animals they like, not just those in the book. The repetitive words of the animals are quickly picked up by children to help them take on the animal roles. Simple animal masks provide one way to help children get more involved in the roles. One six-year-old, upon hearing the story, got out his odd assortment of homemade and bought animal puppets—a rabbit, an elephant, an alligator ("which is the right color to be the frog"), and a bee ("to be The Long One") and began to act out the story as a puppet play.

Flossie and the Fox by Patricia McKissack

In this Tennessee folktale, Flossie, a young black girl who lives in the rural South, goes through the woods to deliver a basket of eggs. Before she sets out, her mother warns her to be on the lookout for a fox. But Flossie has never seen a fox and when she meets it she won't let it convince her it is a fox. She outwits the fox by comparing each of its characterestics to other friendly forest animals (for instance, its tail is busy like a squirrel's).

Flossie's behavior and wit in dealing with the fox provide an appealing alternative to the behavior of female characters like Little Red Riding Hood or Goldilocks. As with *Who's In Rabbit's House?*, the repetitiveness of this story and language, as Flossie compares the fox with first one and then another animal, helps children become comfortable with the action of the story. They bring elements from the story into their play by pretending to go through the woods on an errand. A basket or container with a handle might serve as a good catalyst to help the play get started.

Where the Wild Things Are by Maurice Sendak

Well-known Max goes around his house in his "wolf suit" making mischief and is sent to his room where he goes on a boat voyage to Where the Wild Things Are. There he becomes king by casting a spell over the scary, but appealing, wild things. The story appeals to the naughtiness and desire for power which many young children feel. The Wild Things provide a wonderfully safe way to be scary and also give children the opportunity to use magical powers (spells as opposed to weapons) to tame scary things.

Children often love to pretend to be The Wild Things, "roaring their terrible roars, gnashing their terrible teeth and rolling their terrible eyes." The role of Max, as king of The Wild Things, is also often enthusiastically acted out. Making an enclosure that suggests a boat (arranging pillows in a boat shape, for instance) and providing a prop that suggests an oar can help the play get started; so can making a simple king's crown out of construction paper.

My Father's Dragon, Elmer and the Dragon and *The Dragons of Blueland* by Ruth Gannett

By about five years old, many children are ready for chapter books which rely more on words than pictures. Such books, with their greater complexity and depth, encourage children to get absorbed with a plot and characters over a period of time and to think about what might happen as they wait for the next sequel. Such an involvement will often carry over to dramatic play. And the absence of pictures leaves a lot to the imagination and can motivate children to put the words into action in dramatic play.

Books like the three in this series provide an excellent place to begin. Told through the eyes of his son, they recount a father's adventures when he was a boy with a friendly dragon. First, he travels to an island to rescue the baby dragon from wild animals who kidnapped it as a baby and are making it work for them; he brings along a knapsack, lollipops, rubberbands, chewing gum, a jackknife and a burlap bag, each of which helps him cope with a danger he meets along the way. In the second book the father takes the dragon on the long journey home to his house. And in the third, they return to the dragon's homeland and save the dragon's family from impending danger. Each book has an imaginary map of the route traveled by the father which can be referred to as the adventure progresses.

Similar in theme to *Where the Wild Things Are* (for younger children) and *The Wizard of Oz* by L. Frank Baum (for older children), these tales capture children's desire to be independent, competent and brave The resourcefulness of the child, the friendship which develops between the boy and the dragon, the graphic and dramatic nature of the dangers they confront and prevail over, all provide powerful content for pretend play. Each book provides its own adventure and can be developed through play. And by the time all three of the books have been read, children are often completely immersed in the lives of the characters and want to keep them going by adding their own adventures.

To help play get started, try suggesting that an area rug become the island and that cardboard circles be set out as the stepping stones that "My Father" walked over to get to the island in the first tale. Stuffed or small plastic animals (lions, tigers, elephants, monkeys— whatever wild animals you have around) can provide a further stimulus. You might also suggest using a backpack or suitcase to pack some of the supplies that served as "My Father's" weapons (like gum, a lollipop and a bag) or help a child develop her own ideas about what she might need to pack.

12
Resources and Organizations

Children's Books

Aardema, Vera. *Who's in Rabbit's house?* New York: Dial Books for Young Readers, 1977.

Barrie, J.M. *Peter pan.* New York: Viking Penguin, 1911.

Baum, L. Frank. *The wizard of Oz.* Chicago: Rand McNally, 1900.

Burningham, John. *Come away from the water, Shirley.* New York: Crowell, 1977.

Galdone, Paul. *The three billy goats gruff.* New York: The Seabury Press, 1973.

Gannett, Ruth Stiles. *My father's dragon.* New York: Alfred A. Knopf, 1948.

———. *Elmer and the dragon.* New York: Alfred A. Knopf, 1950.

———. *The dragons of blueland.* New York: Alfred A. Knopf, 1951.

Greenfield, Eloise. *Me and Neesie.* New York: Crowell, 1975.

Keats, Ezra Jack. *Louie.* New York: Scholastic Book Services, 1975.

———. *The trip.* New York: Scholastic Book Services, 1978.

———. *Regards to the man in the moon.* New York: Four Winds Press, 1981.

Kellogg, Steven. *The mysterious tadpole.* New York: Dial Books for Young Readers, 1977.

McKissack, Patricia. *Flossie and the fox.* New York: Dial Books for Young Readers, 1986.

McPhail, David. *The magical drawings of Moony B. Finch.* New York: Doubleday, 1978.

Potter, Beatrix. *Peter rabbit.* New York: Frederick Warne Picture Books, 1902.

Sendak, Maurice. *Where the wild things are.* New York: Harper and Row, 1963.

Dr. Seuss. *Bartholomew and the Oobleck.* New York: Random House, 1949.

———. *The cat in the hat.* New York: Random House, 1957.

———. *The cat in the hat comes back.* New York: Random House, 1958.

Charlotte Zolotow. *William's doll.* New York: Harper and Row, 1972.

175

Readings for Adults

Auerbach, S. *The toy chest: A sourcebook of toys for children*. Secaucus, NJ: Lyle Stuart, 1986.

Bettleheim, B. "The importance of play." *The Atlantic Monthly*, March, 1987.

Carlsson-Paige, N., and Levin, D.E. *Helping young children understand peace, war and the nuclear threat*. Washington, DC: National Association for the Education of Young Children, 1985.

Carlsson-Paige, N., and Levin, D.E. *The war play dilemma: Balancing needs and values in the early childhood classroom*. New York: Teachers College Press, 1987.

Coles, R. *The moral life of children*. Boston: The Atlantic Monthly Press, 1986.

Coles, R. *The political life of children*. Boston: The Atlantic Monthly Press, 1986.

Damon, W. *The moral child: Nurturing children's natural moral growth*. New York: The Free Press, 1988.

Galinsky, E., and David, J. *The preschool years*. Reading, PA: Addison-Wesley, 1988.

Greenfield, P.M. *Mind and media: The effects of television, video games and computers*. Cambridge, MA: Harvard University Press, 1984.

Judson, S., ed. *A manual on nonviolence and children*. Philadelphia: New Society, 1984.

Mander, J. *Four arguments for the elimination of television*. New York: Quill, 1978.

Oppenheim, J. *Buy me! Buy me!: The Bank Street guide for choosing toys for children*. New York: Pantheon Books, 1987.

Paley, V. *Boys and girls: Superheroes in the doll corner*. Chicago: University of Chicago Press, 1984.

Paley, V. *Bad guys don't have birthdays: Fantasy play at four*. Chicago: University of Chicago Press, 1984.

Peterson, R., and Felton-Collins, V. *Piaget handbook for teachers and parents: Children in the age of discovery, preschool—third grade*. New York: Teachers College Press, 1986.

Strom, D., ed. *Growing through play: Readings for parents and teachers*. Monterey, CA: Brooks/Cole, 1981.

Tuchscherer, P. *TV interactive toys: The new high tech threat to children*. Bend, Oregon: Pinnaroo, 1987. (Distributed by Gryphon House, P.O. Box 275, Mt. Rainier, MD 20712.)

Winn, M. *Unplugging the plug-in drug*. New York: Viking-Penguin, 1987.

Resources

Animal Town Game Company Mail Order Catalog. P.O. Box 2002, Santa Barbara, CA 93120, 805-682-7343. (This Company only includes cooperative and noncompetitive games and toys in its catalog.)

Charren, P., and Hulsizer, C. *The TV-smart book for kids: Puzzles, games and other good stuff brought to you by Action for Children's Television.* New York: E.P. Dutton, 1986.

Crary, E. *Kids can cooperate: A practical guide for teaching problem solving.* Seattle: Parenting Press, 1984.

Fleugelman, Andrew, ed. *The new games book.* Garden City, NJ: Doubleday, 1976.

Fluegelman, Andrew, ed. *More new games and playful ideas.* Garden City, NJ: Doubleday, 1981.

Kreidler, W. *Creative conflict resolution: More than 200 activities for keeping peace in the classroom.* Glencoe, IL: Scott, Foresman, 1984.

Kobrin, B. *Eyeopeners!: How to choose and use children's books about real people, places and things.* New York: Penguin, 1988.

Lipson, E. *Parent's guide to the best books for children.* New York: Times Books, 1988.

Orlick, T. *The cooperative sports and games book.* New York: Pantheon Books, 1978.

Orlick, T. *The second cooperative sports and games book.* New York: Pantheon Books, 1982.

PlayFair Toys. Play Fair, 1690 28th Street, Boulder, CO 80301, 800-824-7255. (Mail-order catalog for nonviolent, nonsexist toys.)

Savanna Books, 858 Massachusetts Avenue, Cambridge, MA 02139. (Mail-order catalog of a wide range of culturally diverse, nonstereotyped books.)

Singer, D. and J. *Make believe—Games and activities to foster imaginative play in young children.* Glenview, IL: Scott, Foresman, 1985.

Singer, D. and J., and Zuckerman, D. *Getting the most out of TV.* Glenview, IL: Scott, Foresman, 1981.

Sobel, J. *Everybody wins: 393 non-competitive games for young children.* New York: Walker, 1983.

Stop War Toys Campaign Packet. Compiled and distributed by New England War Resisters League, Box 1093, Norwich, CT 06360. (Updated annually.)

UNICEF. *Games of the world: How to make them, how to play them, how they came to be.* Zurich, Switzerland: Swiss Committee for UNICEF, 1982. (Available through all local UNICEF distributers and the US UNICEF Committee mail-order catalog.)

Wichert, S. *Keeping the peace: Practicing cooperation and conflict resolution with preschoolers.* Philadelphia: New Society, 1989.

Organizations

Action for Children's Television (ACT)
20 University Road
Cambridge, MA 02138
(617) 876-6620

A nonprofit organization that advocates for diversity in children's television, truth in children's advertising and regulation of TV by the FCC. It distributes a newsletter, books and pamphlets, films and other materials including a speaker's kit and television viewing guide for children.

Center for Psychological Studies in the Nuclear Age
1493 Cambridge Street
Cambridge, MA 02139
(617) 497-1553

This is an interdisciplinary center for research and public education on the psychosocial aspects of the nuclear age. Among its recent projects is the videotape, *The World Is a Dangerous Place,* about the images of friends and enemies portrayed on violent children's television cartoons (available for rental).

Center on War and the Child
P.O. Box 487, Dept. F.
Eureka Springs, AR 72632
(501) 253-8900

The Center's research, education and advocacy activities focus on the victimization of children by civil and international conflict, and the effects of war toys and how to organize against them. It publishes a newsletter and action alerts, and has produced a slide presentation, "Disarming the Children: A Response to the War Toy Industry," which is available for purchase. (Membership: $18)

Children's Creative Response to Conflict (CCRC)
Box 271
Nyack, NY 10960
(914) 358-4601

A national network affiliated with the Fellowship of Reconciliation, CCRC is working to help children learn to cooperate, communicate and deal creatively with conflict. It publishes teaching and parenting materials and a newsletter, and conducts training workshops.

Concerned Educators Allied for a Safe Environment (CEASE)
c/o Peggy Schirmer
17 Gerry Street
Cambridge, MA 02138
(617) 864-0999

A national network of parents, teachers and other advocates of young children working to preserve a world for children to grow up in. Working to educate themselves and the public about global issues and to foster public policy initiatives, one current focus is on promoting anti-war-toys efforts nationwide. Distributes quarterly newsletter. (Membership: $5/year)

Council on Interracial Books for Children (CIBC)
1841 Broadway
New York, NY 10023
(212) 757-5339

The council provides resources to counter racism, sexism and other forms of bias in school and society through its filmstrips, newsletter, curriculum materials, children's book bibliographies and resource center for educators.

Educators for Social Responsibility (ESR)
23 Garden Street
Cambridge, MA 02138
(617) 492-1764

This organization works with educators, students and parents to introduce war and peace curriculums and global education into school systems. It produces and distributes several detailed curriculum guides, videotapes and a journal on peace education issues (kindergarten through high school). It sponsors conferences and provides speakers. (Membership in local and national chapters: $35/year)

National Association for the Education of Young Children (NAEYC)
1834 Connecticut Avenue, NW
Washington, DC 20009
(800) 424-2460

This professional organization of more than 50,000 members provides many resources of relevance to parents including books, pamphlets, posters and the journal, *Young Children*. Local and regional chapters around the country as well as the national office write position papers and advocate for public policy on issues that affect the well-being of young children, sponsor conferences and provide speakers. (Membership: price varies with local chapters)

National Coalition on Television Violence (NCTV)
P.O. Box 2157
Champaign, IL 61820
(217) 384-1920

This group monitors television violence (especially as it relates to children's programming), sends out periodic reports and press releases, and produces a regular newsletter. (Membership: $25/year)

Unitarian Universalist Service Committee
(Boston Area Unit)
78 Beacon Street
Boston, MA 02108
(617) 742-2120

A subgroup is working on anti-war-toy activities and distributes a periodic newsletter with information about what is happening around the world.

War Resisters League/New England (WRL)
P.O. Box 1093
Norwich, CT 06360
(203) 889-5337

The "Stop War Toys Campaign," which is a part of this group, has taken a leadership role in educating and organizing citizens around the country (and internationally) to limit the proliferation of war toys. It prepares and distributes an annual "Stop War Toys Campaign Packet" ($4 plus postage) and "War Toys on the March" leaflet and other useful materials for educating the public. It also provides speakers on war toys and serves as a clearinghouse for groups in the US doing work against war toys.

Index

KEEPING THE PEACE:
Practicing Cooperation and Conflict Resolution with Preschoolers

Susanne Wichert
Foreword by Kathy McGinnis

Keeping the Peace is a handbook for all parents, daycare providers, kindergarten teachers and playgroup leaders striving to create harmonious groups, to bolster children's self-esteem and to foster cooperative, creative interactions between children of 2 1/2 to 6 years old.

The heart of *Keeping the Peace* is its collection of over 35 innovative (and inexpensive) activities, each presented concisely for easy use. These are bolstered by articulate and accessible discussions of the theory behind the design and by anecdotes from the author's journals of her own extensive experience with children.

8 1/2" x 11". 160 pages. Exercises. Bibliography.
Pb $12.95 ISBN 0-86571-158-5
Hb $34.95 ISBN 0-86571-157-7

To order directly from the publisher, add $1.75 to the price for the first copy, 50¢ each additional. Send check or money order to: New Society Publishers, PO Box 582, Santa Cruz, CA 95061, USA.

THE FRIENDLY CLASSROOM FOR A SMALL PLANET:
A Handbook on Creative Approaches
to Living and Problem Solving for Children

Children's Creative Response to Conflict Program

A handy resource book, *The Friendly Classroom* contains exercises and plans which help develop a community in which children are capable and desirous of open communication; enable children to gain insight into their own and others' feelings, capabilities, and strengths; and help each child develop self-confidence about his or her ability to think creatively and prevent and solve conflicts.

As described in *Educational Leadership, Parents Magazine, The New York Times, Instructor,* and *Sojourners.*

8 1/2" x 11". 134 pages. Illustrated. Resource lists. Bibliography. Index.
Pb $12.95 ISBN: 0-86571-129-1
Hb $39.95 ISBN: 0-86571-128-3

To order directly from the publisher, add $1.75 to the price for the first copy, 50¢ each additional. Send check or money order to: New Society Publishers, PO Box 582, Santa Cruz, CA 95061, USA.

A MANUAL ON NONVIOLENCE AND CHILDREN

Compiled and edited by Stephanie Judson
Foreword by Paula J. Paul, Educators for Social Responsibility

"Stephanie Judson's excellent manual has helped many parents and teachers with whom we have worked. An essential part of learning nonviolent ways of resolving conflicts is the creation of a trusting, affirming, and cooperative environment in the home and classroom. This manual has a wealth of suggestions for creating such an environment. We highly recommend it."
—Jim & Kathy McGinnis, Parenting for Peace & Justice
Recommended by *School Library Journal, The Horn Book, Curriculum Product Review, Education Week, Interracial Books for Children Bulletin.*

8 1/2" x 11". 160 pages. Illustrated.
Pb $12.95 ISBN: 0-86571-036-8
Hb $34.95 ISBN: 0-86571-035-X

To order directly from the publisher, add $1.75 to the price for the first copy, 50¢ each additional. Send check or money order to: New Society Publishers, PO Box 582, Santa Cruz, CA 95061, USA.